DEMOCRACY: A LOVE LETTER

A Love Letter

DEMOCRACY:

AND A GUIDE FOR EVERYONE FIGHTING TO SAVE IT

Kelly A. Clancy

Democracy: A Love Letter

©2024 Kelly A. Clancy

Epilogue Publishing

www.epiloguepublishing.com

Brooklyn, New York, United States

Paperback ISBN: 979-8-9906819-0-3

Ebook ISBN: 979-8-9906819-1-0

Cover design by Sarah Flood-Baumann

Interior design by Liz Schreiter

Edited and produced by Reading List Editorial

ReadingListEditorial.com

To Mom and Dad,
for teaching me that this
world is worth fighting for.

ACKNOWLEDGMENTS

Friends, I had two babies over the course of writing this book. If we've talked about this project at all over the past seven years, know that this book exists because you helped me puzzle through all of the different iterations and turns it could take.

First: this book absolutely could not exist without the dedicated, inspiring, hilarious, brilliant activists and organizers who talked with me over the course of four years of research. During the darkest time in our country's history, conversations with you left me in awe of the work you were doing to fight for a more optimistic future for us all. Even while you were busy saving democracy, you took the time to talk to me about it, invite me to your events, and share with me your triumphs and frustrations. Because the world is considerably more hostile to activists now than it was when I started writing, I made the difficult decision not to mention any of my interview participants by name or location, but know that your spirit and wisdom is threaded through every page of this book. Thank you, thank you, thank you. And whatever I get wrong is obviously on me.

The early research for the book was done with the support from the Nancy Weiss Malkiel Scholars Award at the Woodrow Wilson

Foundation (what is now the Mellon Emerging Faculty Leaders Award at the Institute for Citizens and Scholars. The book me took so long they changed the name of the award *and* the organization!). I also had support from the Faculty Development Committee at Nebraska Wesleyan University. Thanks for your support and believing in the project. I also had research help along the way from multiple talented undergraduate research students at NWU. My brother Ben played a pivotal early role in the research for this book, from strategizing ideas to finding literature to support our ideas to conducting interviews. Thanks brother— this book is better because of you.

I also received tremendous support from a wide and wonderful community in the writing and development stage. To everyone who read early drafts—thank you. You made this book better with your kind, funny, incisive comments and insights. Beth, Sara, Brandy, Emlyn, Ashwini, Lisa, Andrea, Lesley, thank you. Selda, in addition to being an early reader, this vision for the book was born on one of our walk-and-talks, so a special thank you for that space. Sarah, thanks for making my playlist better!

Thanks also to friends who have listened to me bounce these ideas around for years—Wendy, Mirya, and Sara were my pandemic writing support group, and those Fridays nights got me through to where I am now. Thanks also to my Epilogue Editing writing community and all of the folks who have participated in AcWriMo circles and writing retreats with me over the past three years—the writing community made such a difference for me! And now AcWriMo2024 will have a new project!

Around the time that the first draft of this book was coming into existence, I had the exquisite good fortune of signing up for one of Janelle Hanchett's writing classes, and I've been a true believer ever since. Janelle, *thank you* for teaching this recovering academic something about the craft of writing, and about why to write anyway, even when it's hard. Thanks also to the dozens of amazing writers I've encountered in Janelle's courses. Your feedback and comradery has sustained me and made me a better writer.

Lindsey Alexander and the team at the Reading List did a fabulous job with the production of this book. You'll notice Sarah Flood-Baumann's incorporation of the Martin font into the front cover and interior design; this typeface is inspired by the remnants of the Memphis Sanitation Strike of 1968.

Leaving academia in the middle of a pandemic to edit, consult, and write full time was one of the scariest decisions I've ever made. My parents, to whom this book is dedicated, have been supportive beyond measure of everything I've ever done, including letting us move in with them during the pandemic, helping watch our kids, and providing the space for a book like this to come into being. Lorraine and Jim, my MIL and FIL, have provided me space in their homes and hearts for this book. Thank you. Also, thank you to my brother Tommy and my sisters-in-law Kimi and Kelly for being all around awesome.

To my three kiddos, my coconuts, you have my heart. You've been along on this book's journey for your whole lives. I hope it makes you as proud as you make me every day, and I hope you never run out of ways to make good trouble in your world.

Finally, Jim. What can I say? Your love is woven through this book, which I know for certain is here because of your unwavering belief that it should exist in the world. From taking the kids on adventures so I could have solo writing retreats to rerouting family road trips to attend protests to reading every draft that I've ever written to helping with the playlist to becoming the book's cheerleader to telling me, when it all seemed too much, "this book must be published." And then reading another draft. Thank you, I love you.

CONTENTS

A Prelude

MAY 2024

A few weeks ago, we met up with some friends at the Metropolitan Museum of Art, subjected the good patrons of the Greek Wing to five kids shrieking "oooh, a bitty bitty bum bum!" and "peeeennnnis!", got an excellent black and white cookie from the William Greenberg Desserts around the corner, hugged our friends goodbye, and piled our sleepy kids on the train for the ride back to Brooklyn.

When we hit Chelsea, a teenager started screaming that a man on the train had a gun and all hell broke loose. The teenager jammed the doors open so the train couldn't leave the station, yelling at the conductor to do something. An elder woman caught my eye and gestured to me to get my kids on the ground, under the train seat. I woke my three-year-old, who was napping in her stroller, and whispered the lyrics to "Skidamarink a Dink a Dink" while trying to hold her crying body still while locking eyes with my older kids, trying to communicate . . . what? "I love you, it'll be okay (I don't know if it'll be okay) stay still, I love you . . ."

A man on the train turned to us: "Look, the guy ran into the tunnel, I don't know when he's coming back but it's safe in the station right now. Get your kids. Go." We flew—tossing the Nintendo Switch and half-eaten Goldfish in the stroller, my daughter on top of that, not buckling her in, running out of the car to find a dozen (more?) NYPD officers standing on the platform, doing . . . nothing. Not looking concerned. Not helping a frantic family of three small children to safety. Not sending officers into the tunnel after the man with the gun. Nothing.

Who helped us that day? The people on the train who saw the gun and yelled for help, holding the door open. The woman who saw me freeze and shepherded my children as her own. The man who stayed, instead of running away because *he* knew it was safe. Not the NYPD, who (when you'd most like cops to be heroes) did nothing. New Yorkers saved each other.

I'm trying to make sense of launching a book about politics in 2024 where I'm feeling confused and heartsick and desperately worried about the future of the country. After using this book as a tool to puzzle over how we make politics better for the better part of a decade, I'm still in awe of (flummoxed by) how much I don't know. There's a great story where the late Chinese premier Zhou Enlai (in conversation with a disgraced US statesman who finally died while I was writing this book) was asked about the impact of the French Revolution, and he said, "It's too soon to say." Some folks have reviewed the transcript from that conversation and surmised that he was in fact talking about the Paris protests of 1968, but I love the story and the sentiment. And it holds my terror at releasing this book into the world now, right when it feels we could be on the brink of another 1968.

My son—he's 10—is in a book club at school where they are reading *Number the Stars*. He came home the other day upset because one of the kids in his class had asked whose side he would be on, and another kid replied that he'd be on the side of the Nazis, arguing that Jewish people don't belong in the United States or in his home country (his family is from the Balkans). In a diverse Brooklyn public school, with Jewish folks as our neighbors and among our closest friends, these conversations are happening at lunch. And with all of our focus on raising anti-racist kids, we didn't see this coming. Anti-Semitic ethnic-cleansing rhetoric, is still alive.

A thoughtfully written essay by Columbia faculty member Bruce Robbins in the *London Review of Books* draws a careful line between out-cry against genocide in Gaza and the Israeli policy of "industrial-scale killing of Palestinians," and threats against Jewish people. We have to keep making that distinction, to ourselves and in public, again and again. Criticizing governments should never be contorted as an existential threat to a group of people. Of course, Republicans (and some Democrats) have neatly framed all pro-Palestinian organizing as anti-Semitic in their zeal to eradicate protest politics from our country.

So, I don't know. In the book, I'm sure I get things wrong. I know that there are tensions and contradictions, places where I skate over hard truths. As much as I want this to feel evergreen, every book is nothing more than an artifact of its moment in time and space. And I'm sure you, with the grace of hindsight and the wisdom of the future, will find parts that feel cringeworthy and outdated because, as I was writing, "it was too soon to say." But there are two things that I hope feel true: people aren't their governments. And we can, and need to, save each other—now more than ever. To paraphrase the lovely Maggie Smith (poet, not actor), with this book I am trying to teach you to love the world.

With love,
Kelly (May 2024)

Introduction:

WE HAVE A WORLD TO SAVE

This is fucked up and we can't mourn alone.

—A DEMOCRACY ACTIVIST FROM CALIFORNIA, 2018

This is a book about creating the world you want to live in. In July 2023, the Supreme Court of the United States ruled that a website designer could refuse services to a (fictitious, as it turns out) gay couple based on "religious" beliefs. In her searing dissent, Justice Sonia Sotomayor wrote:

> I fear that the symbolic damage of the Court's opinion is done. But that does not mean that we are powerless in the face of the decision. The meaning of our Constitution is found not in any law volume, but in the spirit of the people who live under it.

One of the nine people tasked with spending the rest of their lives interpreting the Constitution did something remarkable here: she set it free, entrusting it to the "spirit of the people." How do we live up to the spirit of the Constitution, and save democracy in the process? As busy people, with busy lives, how can we make our part of the world live up to our ideals? The answer to this question is at the heart of this book.

This moment needs all of us because, frankly, the world is on fire. In 2020, the widely respected Varieties of Democracy report warned that the United States, a long-standing liberal democracy, "is only a fraction away from losing this status after substantial autocratization." In other words, we have only years—at best—to save our democracy. The problem is global: in 2011, 49 percent of the world's population lived in an autocracy.[1] Today, 70 percent does. There are only 34 liberal democracies left in the world, a number that appears to be trending downward.

Electing Democrats isn't enough to save us. We need to be our own heroes.[2] Many people yearn for the "no drama Obama" days. But, whether it's banning books, denying trans kids the right to health care, repealing abortion rights, or lying to the public about stolen elections, the past few years have shown us that the far-right has no shortage of plans for taking over our schools, health care, and democracy—we can't sleep on it or expect that voting for and donating money to progressive candidates is enough. Electing Democrats is *necessary* to getting ourselves out of this, but it sure isn't *sufficient.*

Every time something makes you mad politically—on the local, state, or national level—it's because the other side out-organized. We need to know that Republicans are organizing all of the time, pouring millions of dollars into think tanks that are their organizing apparatuses (apparati?).[3] We need to out-organize the other side.[4]

But the good news is, we've gotten pretty good at winning. Electorally, we won in 2017. We won in 2018 (which some people have compared to 1968 in terms of its cultural and historical significance). We won in 2019. We won in 2020. We kept the Senate and battled Republicans to a draw over the House in 2022, channeling national rage over the Dobbs decision to the ballot box. In 2024, we even won back George Santos's seat. This has saved democracy for another day and changed the face of organizing and activism in our country.

This book is a combination love letter and how-to guide: a love letter to everyone who has struggled to make this country a more just, democratic place to live and a how-to guide for people who want to participate but aren't sure how.

How to Use This Book

At the back of the book is a section entitled the "After Party," which provides (brief) historical context for what you're reading. From time to time, you'll encounter [📢], which is a signal that you can flip to the back and read more if you're hazy on the facts. If your history feels a little rusty, the After Party can help.

Finally, the book comes with a playlist for each section. At the beginning of each chapter is a QR code that you can scan, and it'll take you to the Spotify playlist with some tunes that will hopefully give you something to hum along with as you make plans to save the world.

This is your invitation to start showing up: our democracy depends on people participating in progressive social movements focused on advancing, as social movements expert Donatella Della Porta said, "an inclusive vision of a just society and . . . deepening democracy." And it's more than that, to me, and I suspect to you as well. As James Baldwin said: "*The bottom line is this: You write in order to change the world, knowing perfectly well that you probably can't.*"

I want to change the world. I want you to write, march, show up, so we can change the world together. But—I'm not trying to convince you to floss or do your taxes. What I propose is a *slow* (and fun and meaningful) approach to organizing. Showing up is all about deciding to fight back against the stuff that makes you mad, finding people that you like and having them show up with you, and deciding on a mode of action that doesn't make you feel anxious. This book shows you how to do that.

Saving our democracy isn't easy, but it's also far simpler than we think: we need to commit to a strategy of consistent organizing in our communities, have a radically inclusive vision of who organizes with us, and embrace an ethos of slow organizing. After all, it's a marathon, not a sprint. Mass mobilization is a one-trick pony: useful at times, but not the only form of activism that is effective. This moment needs *you* to be involved because you belong to this movement. This belonging isn't just because of your race or place of origin; it's because you share a vision of the world with people who matter. If we can articulate what that world looks like, people will want to join us. This is an invitation to all of you: decide you're going to change the world, and get to work. Here's how we do it.

When We Organize, We Win

Y'all. We fixed acid rain. We closed the hole in the ozone layer. We eradicated polio! We—and, take it from this New York City girl, this is *very* important—figured out how to keep roaches at bay. We don't smoke in restaurants or on planes anymore. You can't buy leaded gasoline! We've made significant (but too slow) progress on most of the UN's Millennium Development Goals. I am *not* saying we're done, or that we've done enough. But I *am* saying that the reason that politicians decided to legislate and budget money to solve these problems, the reason scientists decided to turn their attention to their problems, is because of the work of activists.

And activists decided to show up after the 2016 election. The 2017 Women's March was the largest protest event in American history, only to be crushed in size by the protests following George Floyd's murder in 2020.[5] Twenty-six million Americans (!!) participated in the protests for Black lives—almost 8 percent of the US population. To put that in perspective, nearly a third of the 81 million people who voted for Biden participated in this march (I'm assuming they were mostly Biden voters, but the world is weird—there may have been some Trump fans in the mix, marching for Black lives). These high-profile protests were the loud, public face of the organizing happening all over the country.

And yet, no one was telling the story of these voters. In 2016, the *New York Times* ran a piece entitled: "How Turned Off Are Voters?

Check Out Tommy's Diner," where angry Ohioans were given space to rant about the looming election. This became part of a new genre of article: diner profiles of "real" America, where "hidden" red voters eat their omelets and complain about taxes.

This was part of a persistent narrative (since thoroughly disproven) that economic anxiety—not racial resentment—drove people to the polls to vote against Hillary Clinton.[6]

The narrative also seemed to go one way, assuming that Democrats needed to reach out to Republicans to understand "real" America, framing and defining "real" America as White and aggrieved (even when a *majority of the American public* had voted for Clinton). As I read these interviews, I was struck by the assumption that these were the voters the media presumed we didn't know. But what about protesters? Where were the diner interviews of the newly mobilized, of those organizing on behalf of the majority of individuals, who had, in fact, voted for Clinton, then gone on to participate in the largest set of protests in American history?

Driven by a desire to tell those stories, I set out to interview the activists whose voices you'll hear throughout the book. And what I found was remarkable: a strategy that preserved democracy and kept authoritarianism at bay. Despite Republican control over both chambers of Congress and the presidency from 2016 to 2018, the Resistance virtually shut down Congress. They famously saved the Affordable Care Act (ACA).[7] A few of their prioritized battles—most vividly, the Kavanaugh confirmation to the Supreme Court—were lost, but then they capitalized on that to mount an unprecedented Blue Wave in the midterms. Protests mattered: researchers found that places with Black Lives Matter protests saw a 15- to 20-percent decrease in police homicides, preventing hundreds of deaths (Campbell 2021).

On January 6, 2021, we witnessed the final electoral victories for the Trump-era resistance. The Georgia Senate races had, improbably, produced two runoff elections—both of which, even more improbably, went to Democrats, handing control of the Senate to Democrats.

Democrats had a governing trifecta: the House, the Senate, and the presidency. This stunning accomplishment was overshadowed by the January 6 insurrection and coup attempt. [🔊]

However, these victories were not without cost. As I was writing this book, Heather Heyer was killed in Charlottesville. As I was writing this book, the Proud Boys were beating activists in Portland and New York City. [🔊] As I was writing this book, Black men affiliated with Ferguson kept turning up dead. As I was writing this book, professors were being targeted and fired for the articulation of progressive ideas in the classroom. In the United States during the age of Trump, the risks of activism were not hypothetical. It was a dangerous time and activists put their bodies on the line for their beliefs. This activism was happening in real spaces, with real consequences.

My Readers, the Resistance, and Me

*The outrage grows.
continues and grows.*

—A MEMBER OF THE RESISTANCE FROM NEW ENGLAND, 2018

At its core, the book is a how-to guide: how to think about democracy, how to organize, how to build community, how to mobilize, how to tell stories, how to sustain momentum. But what do I know about these things? To the extent I have anything new to offer, it comes from my own experiences, smart things that activists shared with me, and smart things that I've read. You'll find those woven throughout the text: my experience, voices of activists, and the thoughts of various experts on social movements.

One of the activists you'll meet a little bit later in this book is Clementine, a mom of two from the Northwest with a mouth like a sailor. At the end of our first conversation, Clementine asked me if I had kids, and I told her about my son and daughter, who were four years old and nine months at the time. She paused, then said: "Don't show your daughter pictures of Trump. Keep her beautiful brain pure for a while longer before she has to see the face of the enemy." Even though the spectre of this man obviously permeates this book, you'll notice his name only comes up sparingly, either in direct quotes or talking about electoral outcomes.[8] This is not a book about him or his presidency—it's a book about you, about us, and the kind of country we can and should build together.

Who Should Read This Book?

As I was writing this book, I had a vision in mind of three (overlapping) groups of people I hope will read it. First, I imagined groups of people all over America getting mad (or feeling optimistic about this moment for change!), deciding to do something about it, and then picking up this book to help them change the world. This is a book club book—buy a copy for friends, drink wine, eat really good cheese, and plot how to save your corner of the world.

Second, I envisioned the people I interviewed, and the millions like them who marched, organized, were arrested, and sacrificed themselves for the movement. I want people to read this book and see themselves in the stories and to have documentation of the activism they participated in over four years.

Finally, I hope scholars of progressive movements to find this book helpful. This book started out as an academic project, and I benefited from countless scholars of democracy and social movements who have systemically studied this topic over the years. I have mostly endnoted the scholarly contributions and insights that the book draws from so people who are interested can follow the academic conversations there while not disrupting the narrative.

Am I an Activist?

When my daughter was born in October 2017, I was gifted a tiny hand-knit pink pussy hat. I would strap her into her baby carrier and tuck her little head into the hat. We were a walking symbol of resistance (so I thought). At one happy hour, a woman approached our table. "You're just a great mom—" she was effusive, I guess more than a few drinks into happy hour "—I know you're going to teach your daughter not to take any shit. From presidents or any other men."

We laughed with her, finished our drinks, and then went to pay, only to find our bill had been settled. "That lady really liked you guys, I guess," the bartender said. It had been quite a while since a stranger had bought my drinks, and I was proud of the solidarity my daughter's little hat inspired.

My activism took many forms over the course of the research for this book. I donated money, attended protests, hosted, or cohosted a few activist events in my town of Lincoln, and sponsored teach-ins at my university. I attended over 25 events across the country over the four years. My two older kids have both been to over a dozen protests (my youngest, born during COVID, and in the era where cars drive over protesters with impunity, has not yet joined any). My brother Ben was pepper-sprayed protesting for the removal of the Silent Sam statue at UNC-Chapel Hill, where they were a graduate student at the time. [📢] My brother Tommy left his appellate law job in Los Angeles for a role with the ACLU of Texas, where he litigates for voting and abortion rights. My parents became frequent features on the local Austin news protesting the travel ban and published multiple op-eds opposing Texas's complicity in the Trump administration. I had students threatened with deportation. I had friends who were arrested.

Importantly, I also strived to become a better advocate and ally over the course of this time. I interviewed a trans organizer who articulated for me the reason pink pussy hats were problematic: as a symbol of the Woman's March, they symbolically equated womanhood with the possession of a (pink) pussy. To them, it felt like a sea of TERFs (trans-exclusive radical feminists). That was enough for me to reassess our wardrobe—I quietly put Emilia's little pink hat away, and rethought about how I performed my race and gender through my activism.

The Voices in This Book

Throughout the book, you'll encounter what I call "Dispatches from the Field," which provide closer looks at the people and organizations that are the connective tissue of organizing in this country. I spent 2017–2020 trying to document and capture the spirit of rebelliousness in the United States (what John Lewis of course calls good trouble). This research is based on a total of 111 long-form interviews with 44 activists from across the country, who agreed to speak with me multiple times over the course of the Trump administration. By checking in with the same activists over three years, I tracked how they maintained their energy to keep fighting, how they adapted to the changing terrain of American politics, and how their movements evolved in relation to one another over time.

I also attended more than 25 activist events across the country, including community building meetings in Philadelphia, a Close the Camps rally in Idaho Falls, Black Lives Matter (BLM) protests in Lincoln, and a pop-up anti-ICE (Immigration and Customs Enforcement) protest in Houston.[9]

These interviews offer a glimpse into the lives of activists in America in the twenty-first century. The youngest participants were in their early twenties, while the oldest were well into their eighties. I interviewed members of Black Lives Matter who became involved because of Ferguson and a Sikh organizer motivated by the murders at the Oak Creek Temple in Wisconsin in 2012. I interviewed Indigenous activists focused on long-term sustainability and environmental issues. I interviewed many White people, some of whom had protested in the 1960s and others who were organizing for the first time.

None of the activists of color I interviewed joined the Resistance or were mobilized because of the 2016 election: all had been active *before* the election. The White activists were more divided: some had been involved in more systemic work, such as abortion access, LGBTQIA+ advocacy, and harm reduction initiatives. Others had been involved in more mainstream health care and Democratic Party organizing or had protested in the 1960s and 1970s.

I felt real connections with the activists I interviewed throughout the book. In 2018, as I did follow-up interviews, it felt like reconnecting with old friends.[10] Tanisha, a member of Black Lives Matter who you'll meet later in the book, had moved across the country to live with her daughter. "I wish you'd called me before the midterms! I was freaking out! It was amazing to see the country was trying to do this Blue Wave," she said. [📣] She was so excited about the results, energized about politics, but also knew the costs, and it was clear that all her eggs were not in a political basket. "I don't know if politics is the road to freedom," she mused to me.

All the participants in this book are referred to by the primary issue they organize around, and I blurred their location within 500 miles. This was upon the request of some participants who felt their safety was increasingly compromised by their activist work, and despite the request by some participants to be referred to by name so their organizations could receive well-earned credit. Participants in 2020 increasingly described feeling like they were in danger. For the first time in her life, one Black Lives Matter activist got spooked by voice messages saying they would "fucking kill her." She didn't know how they had gotten her cell phone number or whether they knew her address. Another participant's husband lost his job after he was arrested in a demonstration at the US Capitol. One activist noticed drones flying over their heads at protests, taking pictures of everyone there. Yet another had her picture circulated by White nationalists in the area, who were doing rolling roadblocks.[11]

These facts made me decide to use pseudonyms throughout the book—primarily to protect the identities of people who had chosen to talk to me about their time organizing. My participants were also limited by their subjectivity and by their own limited perspective of the world. Providing anonymity allowed my participants to be honest about their organization's failings and room for me to provide a more critical perspective on many of the contributions in the book. There are also broader reasons not to use the names of specific people and organizations: you can imagine these stories playing out in your own hometown; you can become the hero in your own corner of America.

The "Dispatches from the Field" boxes share the stories that I learned from these protesters and organizations, giving you a deeper look into why people decide to get involved, and how they organize to make real change.

A final note—in the interviews that are represented here, you'll encounter some coarse language. I kept these quotes verbatim because that's how my participants spoke, and because the world gives us a lot to swear about. As the United Automobile Workers (UAW) president Shawn Fain said in 2023 during their historic strike for better wages and fair working conditions, "We may be foul-mouthed, but we're strategic. We may get fired up, but we're disciplined. We may get rowdy, but we're organized." And I have tried to keep that spirit alive in this book. I hope that my more refined readers will understand.[12]

Isn't voting enough?

There is a real tendency in this country to pretend that the parties are somehow, on their face, equal: that Fox News and MSNBC are the same, that Joe Biden and Donald Trump or Barack Obama and George W. Bush were the same. There's a nice sense of symmetry to that. In fact, one of the comments I get most is that I should drop the calls for progressivism[13] and instead focus on democracy building, an activity that both sides of the aisle can be invited to participate in.

Writing like this, I've been told, overplays my hand, makes it polemic instead of neutral, narrows the audience, and excludes 50 percent of the people I could persuade. Also, I'm told, writing a book like this, with explicit calls for progressivism, excludes debate and compromise and discourse and the things that democracy is supposed to be for.

And I hear all of this, I do. But painting me, or this book, as a shill for the Democratic Party is to miss the point. We live in a time of asymmetric polarization: the Republicans are radicalizing, which changes what the "middle" looks like.[14] To invoke the brilliant Rebecca Solnit, voting is a chess move, not a valentine. Right now, the Democratic Party has shown itself to be more willing to embrace the basic tenets that are necessary to preserve our democratic system and ensure that everyone is guaranteed the right to be safe, well, and happy in our country. Republicans, as a party, have consistently chosen to move to the right: primarying their members who try to work with Democrats (though props to John Boehner, who is now living his best life drinking expensive red wine), making voting harder and less inclusive, passing laws to rewrite history so the country's history of slavery is censored to make White kids feel less "guilty" about the past, etc., taking away women's bodily autonomy and then *arresting* them when they cross state lines to exercise their reproductive freedoms, redefining who "counts" as a citizen, and my list could go on.[15]

My point is that I think the parties are the chess pieces that we move around. We demand a radically inclusive democracy. If Democratic politicians organize around that vision, then we partner with them. If Republicans come to embrace that vision, we partner with them. We need a pro-democratic, anti-fascist movement that prioritizes *all* people and their economic and social safety—and that goes beyond partisanship.

In 2023, New York redrew its city council boundaries, significantly shifting the borders of the districts in South Brooklyn where I live (this is the reddest part of the borough—we're in a congressional district with Staten Island, our friends on the other side of the Verrazzano

Bridge, represented by the very conservative Nicole Malliotakis). I was really dismayed by the race for district 43; Susan Zhuang, who ultimately won her race for the city council seat, ran an ugly campaign, first against Wai Yee Chan, her progressive primary opponent, and then against Ying Tan, her Republican general election opponent. Further, she ran to the *right* of Tan, campaigning on a pretty draconian anti-homelessness, pro-law-and-order platform that spoke to none of the priorities or concerns of the progressive wing of the Democratic Party.

On Election Day, I was torn. On the one hand, I'm a pretty "vote blue, no matter who" kind of gal, thinking that we should always support the candidate who at least wants to see democracy survive another day. On the other hand, I didn't *want* to cast my vote for a candidate whose whole campaign strategy conflicted with my values. So in the end, I wrote in the name of her progressive primary opponent, Wai Yee Chan. I wrote the Zhuang campaign an email about why. Did I throw away my vote? In an instrumental sense, yes. But there was no way that I would ever change the tenor of politics in my district by just voting with the crowd, so I took a calculated gamble, and it paid off— Zhuang won anyway, and I voted my conscience. This is what Rebecca Solnit means when she says voting is a chess move.

On the other hand, consider a Jill Stein voter in Michigan in 2016, where the difference between Clinton and Trump was only around 12,000 votes, and Jill Stein, the Green Party candidate, received just over 51,000 votes. In this case, your symbolic chess move helped put democracy in check! Bad idea![16]

Of course I wish for a vibrant multiparty system that allows for dissent and multiple perspectives. This is why, in part, I think we should have a real conversation as a country about proportional representation, as I discuss in the next chapter. We only have to look at Europe to know that a two-party system actually *flattens* debate and opposition. Let's have a center-left party and a Green Party and have a real debate over who can best protect rights while advocating for climate change. Let's have a far-left party and an independence party like the Scottish Nationalist Party and ask voters to decide who can best oversee the country's economic transitions. Falsely propping up a far-right, anti-democratic Republican Party and painting them as moderate in order to pretend this gives voters a choice is a lie. Our system provides no real choice at all: we can only vote Democrat if we want to save democracy.

DISPATCHES FROM THE FIELD 1:
AN EXAMPLE FROM SCOTLAND

Other countries engage in national conversations somewhat regularly, either as a top-down or bottom-up initiative. The United States, in its fragmented media ecosystem, has dozens of issues, but we tend not to engage in productive discourse about any of them. Here's an example of how it could look. How has a model like this one, built on slow organizing and rethinking inclusivity, played out in other places? For an answer, we look across the Atlantic to Scotland.

In 2014, before all the Brexit turmoil, Scotland held an independence referendum. The referendum was announced in 2013, and there was a 10-month period where the country talked about it deeply. There were conversations, public and private, at schools, in churches, in beer halls. They also allowed 16-year-olds to vote for the first time, arguing that this decision would most profoundly affect the younger generation. The country seriously considered its past, its culture, and its future in the question of whether it should stay as a part of the United Kingdom. In the end, they voted to remain; the ability to be part of both the United Kingdom and Europe was a significant factor in many Scots' decisions.

It was a double blow, then, when the Brexit referendum was announced in February 2016 and happened in June; while Scotland

and Northern Ireland both voted to remain in the European Union, they were outvoted by their English and Welsh counterparts, and the UK began the long process of withdrawing from the EU. I was in Scotland when the Brexit vote happened, and the country felt like it was in a national period of mourning (a prologue to how the United States would feel a few months later). The Scottish voters I talked to lamented that there wasn't time for a real conversation about the stakes of leaving the European Union.

The independence conversation, like the Brexit conversation, was about more than a simple policy choice: it was a question of identity, of culture. When the conversation over Brexit happened so quickly, the economic arguments (which turned out to be false) ruled the day. It's easy to look at numbers and see the cost of either being part of or leaving the EU. What's harder is to have a conversation about the historical role of the European Union as an instrument of peace, as a commitment to humanity beyond nationalism, or what it means to be part of a political body that commits to a way of life and a way of governance for everyone in its borders. People needed more time to develop arguments, to debate these points, and to allow these issues to sink into their psyches.

The timeline didn't give them a chance to have a genuine, national conversation that was separate from politics and politicians. For the independence referendum, they were able to talk deeply to each other for a long time, slowly: that they went beneath the surface, had conversations politicians were not privy to, or were not focused on, and then came back with their minds made up. Although the vote in 2014 revealed a split within the country (55–45), nearly 80 percent turned out, including those 16-year-olds. There was nearly a year between when the referendum was called and when it was held. People talked to each other. They had conversations around dinner tables, in schools, in supper clubs and coffee shops and public forums. Allowing 16-year-olds to vote meant that conversations were happening in high schools, and then kids came home to their parents. There was a concern that students would just vote the way of their parents, but that seemed not to be the case.

There was a sense of satisfaction with the results. There was a question proposed, a conversation about it, and a vote—this did not resolve the issue, or the underlying reasons for the vote, but it made it better—it was a clear example of deep, deliberative democracy at play. Brexit, with its rushed project, betrayed all of that. But we can learn lessons of slow, inclusive organizing from the Scots and their debate over their future.

Slow Organizing: A Model

In 2018, I was living in Lincoln, Nebraska, teaching political science at a small liberal arts school and deep into chronicling protests and collecting stories. On the first Tuesday in November, I told my four-year-old son Sorin it was time for us to go vote in the midterms. There was a surprisingly optimistic bubble around Lincoln—in 2018, Medicaid expansion was on the ballot in Nebraska (it passed in a landslide), and in May 2019, we would elect a truly progressive mayor. Things were looking up: it felt like maybe a little of the Blue Wave was cresting our way. Sorin bounded downstairs, excited and out of breath. "Okay, Mama! Ready to go!" He was wearing a bowtie and carrying the "Families Belong Together" sign we'd made to bring to protests that summer. "We're just going to vote, kiddo," I told him. He grinned. "I know, but you always have to be dressed and ready, just in case a protest breaks out!" Slow organizing is a little bit like that—keep your special protesting bowtie and sign on hand just in case you stumble into a protest as you're going about your day.

There's a quote that I've seen attributed variously to Senator Ed Markey and MacArthur Genius award winner Deborah Meier: when comparing democracy and rocket science, rocket science is harder. I thought about that a lot when writing this book—talking to people about democracy, listening to all the different ways people try to save democracy and then get frustrated, burned out, frozen out of the system. Watching authoritarian regimes emerge and take hold of and invade countries I've visited and loved, and then worrying about the fate of democracy here at home. Seeing the promise of real democracy working in places like Ireland and Scotland, people fighting for a democratic future in Ukraine.[17] In the pages that follow, I don't prescribe a definitive path to a more democratic future, but I do offer some basic precepts: it should be unflinchingly multiracial and anti-patriarchal we should consider proportional representation, and we should embrace economic justice. These should be nonseverable and nonnegotiable. Max Berger, who writes a lot of smart things about politics, had this to say on Bluesky: "One of my firmest, most consistent beliefs is that those of us who oppose ethno-nationalism and authoritarianism around the world need to make an explicit case for how multiracial democracy benefits working people" (@maxberger, November 27, 2023). Yes!

There are also many things we *shouldn't* do if we want to achieve a sustainable democratic future. One is to blame partisanship as the root of all ills. Could we live in a future where we have multiple parties, each offering vibrant but competing visions of how we achieve the goals above? Surely. In fact, many countries around the world have multiparty democracies with a variety of parties that do just that—and they build vibrant coalitions to help advance competing goals legislatively (although many of these same countries still struggle with authoritarianism—without organizing, there's no silver bullet). We don't live in that world.

This book offers an action plan. I'm hoping you'll use it to help fill in the *what*. You dream of the country you want to live in, and then you use this book to help you build it. Before we get into the good stuff—how to save the world and have fun doing it—I'll tell you about the ethos behind the book, the theory of change if you will. I have three guiding principles (the CSI):

1. Organizing requires people to be consistently resisting (C).
2. Our approach to organizing should be *slow.* (S)
3. Our orientation to organizing should be radically inclusive, providing spaces for everyone to thrive. (I)

You'll see these three ideas woven through each step. I set them up here so you can always turn back to this page to remind yourself of the theory guiding the book.

We should be consistently resisting: Right now, we often see activism (as opposed to organizing) as a spigot. When we're mad about something, we call our friends, grab our signs, find a protest to join—or at least retweet something barbed. The rest of the time, we live our normal, nonactivist lives. If we're going to save the country, this needs to shift: we need to be low-level badasses all the time. You'll see examples throughout the book, but the guiding principle is to always be prepared to organize (keep your bowtie and your sign at the ready). This is a mindset as much as it is about doing things—it's about looking for injustice and knowing that you can do things to challenge it. It's about gumming up wheels of power. Sometimes, it's about making an asshole's day a little bit worse instead of better.

How do we know that this works? Because of rats—and science. In the book *Burnout,* written in 2020 by identical twin sisters Emily and Amelia Nagoski, they talk about the psychological impact of impossible tasks on rats. When rats are put in a maze where they can't possibly get the cheese, they stop trying (developing learned helplessness) even when the task becomes possible again (the cheese is moved right around the corner, but the rats won't search it out). But if you do something instead (like moving the rat toward the cheese) then the learned helplessness starts to fade. Our little rat friends develop hope. So, what do the Nagoski sisters recommend? Doing "anything that isn't nothing." That's right—microaction can help you stave off the feelings of despair and helplessness.

If we're always on medium alert, then it means we have time to take breaths as well—to slow down, do some research, read books and be silly and see plays and remind ourselves what's great about our communities and why they're worth fighting for. A lot of what you'll read in this book is about the four exhausting years of mobilizing to resist and defeat the rising authoritarianism that occurred from 2017 to 2020. This kind of approach to organizing was, arguably, the only way democracy could be protected during this time. It also drew a slew of fair criticism. Going full tilt leads to burnout. It means there's an issue of the week and you can't focus on any one thing. There's no time for learning about policy or history or people or for building genuine relationships. Sometimes, we need that kind of energy. Other times, though, we need to invent new speeds for ourselves—what I'm calling slow organizing. During the week, you might go full speed from work to soccer practice to parent-teacher meetings to doctor's appointments. But you don't stop being a parent on the weekend. You just slow it down. It's a softer, kinder, more relaxed version of your identity. The same thing with activism. Sometimes, we elect a fascist and need to go full speed. But then we can't just disengage. We need to be able to pivot to slower activism.

It's not easy. It's easier to disappear into your own safe space, with your own safe people. But finding your allies and committing to a core set of principles—multiracial democracy and mutual economic principles—and building an identity together means that we keep showing up. It means we build relationships, not contacts or networks. It means that even when there is struggle, we cooperate, because the alternative is to defect, which leaves us all poorer. In fact, as political scientists Steven Levitsky and Daniel Ziblatt write in 2023, the need for a multiracial democracy is existential: "Either America will be a multiracial democracy or it will not be a democracy at all." There is no "Herrenvolk democracy": such a thing is a myth. But the good news is this: if we're all consistently resisting, it leaves more time for all of us to rest.

The resistance needs to be slow: A slow organizing approach to mobilization means that we are thinking about how different time horizons fit together in this struggle. We need people who plan giant marches and those who have conversations in basements after town meetings and living rooms after religious services. We need people who plan deep canvassing and slow conversations in the community that are meant to build consensus around issues over a long period of time. We need to not let the frenetic pace of politics determine the timeline of our struggle for freedom. To use a sports metaphor, we're all the same squad, but we have different positions to play—and this is just as true for our job in the movement as it is for our strategy of change. If we're all on the same page in terms of outcomes, we can be on different pages in terms of the path it takes to get there. In fact, it's probably good if we are on different pages because it is important to have diffuse organizing matrixes.

Slow mobilizing also means, as I'll talk about later, letting people take breaks and knowing that they'll come back. It means—White people—showing up in the off-season to do the more systemic work, knowing that you'll be able to pivot to the more episodic work again come election season and that you won't be co-opted by mercenary political parties.

Later in the book, I talk about the incredible strength that is emerging from labor organizing in the country right now. But here, I just want to highlight one thing. The contract that the UAW won expires on April 30, 2028. Do you know why? Shawn Fain, the president of the UAW, negotiated the end date to lay the groundwork for a coordinated May 1 strike should the corporate elites choose to play hardball again. Fain wrote this in a message to members: "We invite unions around the country to align your contract expirations with our own, so that together we can begin to flex our collective muscles. If we are going to truly take on the billionaire class and rebuild the economy so that it starts working for the benefit of many, it's important not only that we strike, but that we strike together." My friends, this is a masterclass in slow organizing.

The resistance needs to be radically inclusive: The third element that's necessary for this to work is a commitment to radical inclusivity, or what I'm calling a universal design for organizing. The type of people you invite to your table determines the type of organizing you do, and folks with disabilities, nonwhite folks, and folks with caring responsibilities are often excluded from the proceedings.

This model—one where we are always resisting, we take a slow approach to organizing, and we think about a universal framework for participation and inclusivity—can transform the way we approach organizing spaces. Some of the organizers I talked with spent a lot of time dreaming about how to make it easier for other people to organize. Before COVID, one organizer from California helped establish a childcare collective so marginalized parents could organize. Another talked about brainstorming positions that people of different abilities could excel in: "Direct organizing work was going to be too very traumatizing and also too physically draining for me, but the education work was something where I had both the skill and the excitement." And this is the crux of what I believe: saving this country is the project of our lives. And it's a big enough project that everyone can—needs to—play a transformative role.

We Can Save the World

A few words about what you'll find in the next four chapters. Each chapter explores a step in the process of slow organizing. It presents a practical list of things you can do and—and not do—to organize in your community.

Slow organizing involves finding your people, mobilizing them, embedding your movement in the community, and envisioning a future that works for everyone. This is the framework for the rest of the book, chapter by chapter.

Step One: Envision a Democratic Awakening. What kind of democracy do you want to live in? This step offers 13 ideas for how to build institutions that work for everyone.

Step Two: Find Your People. This step focuses on finding your "why": deciding why you want to organize, building friendships with people who are also committed to those goals, and nurturing those relationships so they can grow over time.

Step Three: Mobilize (but Slow Your Roll). Organizing can look so many ways—having conversations, opting out of injustice, being selective in how you spend your money and what you consume, staging sit-ins and dance-ins, you name it. Many groups found that having one or two specific activities kept people motivated and coming back. Be flexible enough that people can do lots of different things and have it "count" as organizing; encourage people to play to their strengths and interests. At the same time, make sure there is time for breathing. We are trying to build a better world, and this means time for rest.

Step Four: Sustain Your Momentum. The great thing about community work is that it requires things to be slow. Getting to know your neighbors allows you the time to do deep canvassing work and have conversations about the type of world you want to live in.

It's hard to do this. Public spaces are increasingly hard to find. The talk radio and podcast world of misinformation makes it harder to have a conversation as members of a community. But you're building the community you want your family to live in.

DISPATCHES FROM THE FIELD 2:
IRELAND'S GAY MARRIAGE AND ABORTION MIRACLE

Grassroots activism works to produce national change. Take this example: Ireland successfully legalized gay marriage in 2015 and abortion in 2018 via referendum. Whereas we see rights extended to minoritized communities via top-down change (through courts or legislatures) in many other countries, Ireland put the questions to its people. In 2015, nearly two-thirds of voters approved a referendum to legalize gay marriage; this included a high-profile "home to vote" campaign, where Irish citizens from all over the globe returned home to vote "yes." Even more remarkably, Ireland was the first country in the world to approve gay marriage via popular vote.

Three years later, in 2018, activists achieved yet another victory, when 66 percent of the country voted to legalize abortion in the country. (Interestingly enough, this is the same percentage of people voting for a women's right to abortion in states from Kansas to Michigan in the aftermath of the Supreme Court overturning of *Roe v. Wade*. [📢])

In 2018, I traveled with two students to Ireland to interview the activists who were part of the movement to legalize gay marriage and abortion in the country. We were struck by the fact that it was the *same people* who were behind both initiatives: they planned it as a five-year campaign, beginning to build momentum first around gay marriage and a focus on love. This created the permission structure to move the national conversation to a focus on abortion. And, they won—by building coalitions, having real conversations with people across the country with whom they could find common ground, and by doing the hard work of organizing.

Step One:

ENVISION A DEMOCRACY THAT WORKS

DISPATCHES FROM THE FIELD 3:
MEET TANISHA

Tanisha was an organizer for Black Lives Matter from the Northeast who moved to the West Coast after a series of death threats. Her conversations were integral in helping structure my thinking about this book. Here is her story:

I always have been an activist really since I was 16; but what really got to me was when I went to Ferguson after Mike Brown was murdered. I would tell my boss "I feel like something has to be done. I feel hopeless. I need to be in Ferguson." She was like, "Well, just go." Going into Ferguson and going on to Canfield Drive where he was killed just took me to another level. When I got back, I decided to cofound a BLM chapter. But I've always been a staunch advocate, I remember just being as a kid and when my mom would say things, I was like, "That doesn't sound right, that seems unfair." It's always been in my heart, but I just always tell people Ferguson kinda kicked me up to another level of . . . I don't like to use the word radical, because people think it's so bad . . . but I like to just be a "liberation person." I was like, you know, we have to be as Black people liberated and have freedom and justice over our bodies, over our autonomy. I would say that's been about four or five years ago that kicked me to another level of "Let's get this started." Trayvon Martin is the one that really got the name hashtag out, but I always tell people that I think BLM became really to me a very large, visible organization when Mike Brown was murdered. For me, my activism has always been about how Black people get a seat at the table of policymakers that make policies that impact us negatively. I mean, I always tell people for every policy that you make, if you're not doing it under an anti-blackness lens, it always impacts us negatively.

I tell people you have to have that in your head every time you're doing work, and I've become a lot more vocal about it now. But I've really become more like calling out senators, calling out people running for office, and especially Democrats. I'm real clear that either party, they kill all Black people because I think capitalism makes it bad for us; however, Black people tend to vote Democrat."

Václav Havel's revolutionary essay "The Greengrocer" opens with a line that resonated in my head during the summer of 2020: "A spectre is haunting Eastern Europe: the spectre of what in the West is called 'dissent.' This spectre has not appeared out of thin air."[1] As the world watched the American people take to the streets, it was hard not to feel a glimmer of hope that the same spectre had decided to haunt our country as well.

On May 25, 2020, George Floyd was murdered by a Minneapolis police officer. Darnella Frazier, a brave bystander, caught it on her phone, and the world watched as George Floyd cried out for his mother and then took his last breaths. The world exploded into protests against police violence. Night after night in early June, people took to the streets. For the first time in history, the White House went dark. There was wave after wave of protest. It felt to me like we were finally seeing what American activism was capable of, and it was an incredible feeling. Social media was filled with images of students whose graduation ceremonies were canceled, showing up to protest in caps and gowns.

I was in the surreal place of observing from afar: In late April, I gave birth to my third child. In June, we took a "covidcation" to go hiking, and our two-year-old daughter slipped off a cliff. My husband Jim dove after her and caught her, and was life-flighted to a hospital in a neighboring state. Our daughter walked away with a few minor bruises. Rather than being on the frontlines of these protests, which part of me had waited my entire life to join, instead I followed the events from a COVID/postpartum/hospital fever dream as Jim spent weeks in the critical care section of the trauma unit, praying that he would survive and that my tiny baby wouldn't contract COVID (we were lucky on both counts).

Once we were back home, I touched base with everyone I knew in the movement who struggled to explain the protests; one said: "Maybe God just decided to do us a favor: 'Yeah, here's your disease, and here's your smoke, and here's your Four Horsemen of the Apocalypse. By the way, folks are going to notice structural racism.'" These protests showed the awesome power of this country to mobilize against violence and oppression.

COVID also kept many activists in their homes, which reshuffled the balance of power of who was able to come out to protest. As Tanisha told me:

> Black people are always resisting. This time, the comrades and allies have become part of the Resistance. Before, when we were out in the streets people would be like 'there they

go again' . . . . But this time, it's clear that this is a police state and people said 'hell no.' This time our comrades have stayed in the streets with us, have been arrested, and have gotten arrested so we don't get arrested and that's how the uprising works. That's how it's supposed to work—even people who don't look like us are saying 'this is wrong and we're going to be in the streets with them too . . . and we're going to be the ones to help bail them out. We're going to be the ones to do whatever meets the needs to protect Black people. I love it . . . . *Oh my God, these comrades are doing their thing.*

For a moment, some White people were willing to pay some of what Juliet Hooker calls the burden of citizenship, to notice the structural racism, put their bodies on the line. Reading this should make everyone pause because where we are now feels so far from that moment. If George Floyd was murdered today, what would the country do? If Black people were in the streets, would we see White people mobilizing in front of them, using their bodies in solidarity to take those blows? Or was this one opening, one critical juncture, that has passed?

I don't know. I admit that the lack of protesters in the street after Roe was overturned caught me off guard. The American people are capable of accomplishing great things through protest, but it often feels as though we unilaterally disarm.

In the time that's followed, I've thought about what it means to engage in a true movement from freedom and democracy. Progressives need to unite around a shared articulation of a multiracial democracy based on mutual aid. Although there obviously is no certainty about what that might look like, here are some basic principles and ideas that might be worth having national conversations about. I've struggled with this chapter to avoid being overly prescriptive, because I think that you need to have a conversation about what the specifics should look like.

Instead, this chapter provides guidance about conversations that are worth having, and pitfalls that are worth avoiding. This looks like a re-envisioning of democratic representation that challenges the antidemocratic pillars of our Constitution. This looks like radical inclusion, and a politics of identity based on radical inclusion as well as a focus on intersectionality. Finally, this looks like mutual aid and (democratic) socialism, and an economic system that taxes capital and genuinely invests in people. A narrative of radical inclusivity needs to call people in for tough conversations, but also make them feel like they belong. Belonging isn't just because of your race or place of origin; it's because you share a vision of a world. If we can articulate what that world looks like, people will want to join us in building it. That's the cheesy, optimistic thesis of the book.[2]

13 Ways to Change the System

People say "the system is broken" a lot, and I used to think that was true. I've changed my mind about this over the years. Today, I think that the system isn't broken—it's working as designed. Tanisha was careful to make the distinction between whether our political system was broken, or whether it was in fact working as designed: "We know that this needs to be dismantled real quick, but the system is working the way it's supposed to work. It's not broken—the way it's working intentionally doesn't work for Black and Brown folks." In a system that is designed to fail, it is particularly difficult to support democracy wholeheartedly.[3]

Let's take the example of the embarrassing lack of affordable childcare in this country. A lot of people point to it as a broken system. But indeed, we *almost* had universal childcare in the 1970s—and Nixon vetoed it after sustained conservative pressure (the bill was communist, Republicans claimed). So the system is working the way Republicans designed it: to hurt children, families, and the country's trust in good governance.

However, we can and should work within institutions as one of the levers of power that are available to us. Sitting out electoral politics is willingly giving up our ability to access change: decreasing the number of ways that activists can link themselves to the state.[4]

The good news is, there are political models that work pretty well. Multiracial, social(ist) democracy is the recipe for the future. Social(ist) democracies in Europe need to learn how to preserve their welfare state in a multiracial and ethnic future. Activists in neoliberal, austerity-driven countries like the United States need to learn how to make an argument for a socialist democracy that is radically inclusive. We need to articulate a vision of these three pillars as inseparable: democracy, radically inclusive (multiracial and anti-patriarchal), and socialist.

Movements are what happen when traditional democratic channels shut down: we all should be planning to organize our way to resistance, but not to quit until all of us are free. Organizing is complicated, and as we're all engaged in a struggle for liberation, we should allow it to happen at different cadences and with different messages. The brilliant Michelle Alexander wrote in the *New York Times* "The disorienting nature of Trump's presidency has already managed to obscure what should be an obvious fact: viewed from the broad sweep of history, Donald Trump is the Resistance. We are not." However, we all know that those of us who care about this country—and about progressive values more broadly—are going to be engaged in struggle for the rest of our lives.

Republicans are traditionally very good at defining through exclusion who "counts" for things—and then creating a club that you want to be part of so that you aren't excluded too. Nowhere is this truer than over the "family values" and "parental choice" movements. Who decides *which* families and *which* parents? Why is my family, which is pro-reproductive freedom, pro-civil and human rights for everyone across gender or sexuality, pro-grappling with the complexities and deep shame of our nation's history and how that has determined our present, pro-redistribution of resources so that everyone can live a happier, healthier life—why are those not core family values? I read a sentence the other day about a book ban in Florida or Kentucky or Texas that said something to the effect of "due to the focus on parental choice, books with LGBTQI characters have been taken out of libraries," and I wanted to scream. I'm a parent—that's not my choice! I want my kids to have access to those books, whether they act as a bridge, a mirror, a window, or a sliding door for my kids. And I am absolutely convinced most Americans agree with me, that I represent the "real" America. So next time a politician tells you that you don't count because you aren't "real" America, declare loudly that this is your country too. We are the better, more optimistic, inclusive version of America.

In 2019, Lara Trump tweeted a county-level map that showed a sea of red with blue dots scattered across. Imprinted on the map were the words "Try to Impeach This." (Just Google it if you don't remember what it looks like.) We're used to seeing this map, or versions of it, as a "neutral" depiction of how Americans vote. The problem is, land doesn't vote: people do. When you look instead at the population-level map, instead of the geographic level, a different picture emerges. Spend a few minutes playing around on the website Engaging-Data.com to see how truly different the country can look.

Democracy should be about people, not about land. At the same time, "small" things like maps have an enormous capacity to shape how we understand people and power.[5]

Here is my mini-manifesto: 13 things we can do to save the world. This isn't meant as an exhaustive list, but instead a set of principles that can guide your organizing and help us figure out what it looks like to live in a functional democracy.[6]

1. Envision a representative electoral system.
2. Envision a robust democracy.
3. F**k the patriarchy.
4. F**k White supremacy.

5. F**k unchecked capitalism.
6. Tell a story about this vision.
7. Rechart your relationship with the Democratic Party.
8. Challenge your theory of change.
9. Run for office.
10. Stop eating our own.
11. Call people in, not out.
12. Take leadership from young people.
13. "Find and replace" what drains your energy.

1. Envision a representative electoral system

When the United States helps new transitional democracies set up governmental institutions, we always suggest some kind of parliamentary democracy with a weak executive, multiple parties, and lots of power sharing. Why? Because when people feel represented by their parties, they tend to buy into the system more. Countries with strong executives and fewer parties tend to be less representative, leading people to feel disenfranchised: this can lead to bad results from coups to massive protests to intractable partisanship.

Of course, the United States is the opposite: we have a strong executive, two parties, and low levels of representation. We need to encourage democratic experimentation, figuring out systems of accountability that might help to create systems where everyone feels like they have a voice.

It often feels as though Republicans are dead set on breaking the electoral system to rig the rules of the game. As one organizer told me: "More so than politics, is the survival of institutions and the republic itself. This is about the end of a functioning democracy; suppressing voters is one thing, but disregarding the will of the voters is another." Broken systems provide opportunities for reinvention as well as repair, but we need to continue to shine the light on places where people are trying to rig the game so that the only Republicans win.

One of the worst (un)intended consequences of our institutional design—the electoral college and first-past-the-post system—is that it eliminates the ability to see activism happening beneath most states' partisan affiliation, even in places where nearly 50 percent of the population votes the other way. A "safe" state is one where 52 percent or so vote the other way (like in Texas)—but that is such a politically demobilizing way of looking at things. Democracy means that all people should have rights and representation.

In a proportional representation (PR) system, the idea is to represent as many people as possible. Let's say a state has ten representatives to send to Congress. The elections are decided, and Democrats win 51 percent of the seats in each of those races, and Republicans win 49 percent. Our system would send 10 Democrats to Congress. Is that the will of the people? No! 49 percent of the people in that state are disenfranchised! That's not fair!

Consider, instead, a PR system with multiple parties, not just two. This time, Democrats win 40 percent of the vote, Republicans 30 percent, Green Party 10 percent, Libertarians 10 percent—who goes to Congress? Four Democrats, three Republicans, one Green Party Member, and one Libertarian. We get real representation. Instead of 49 percent of the population having no representation at all, we get the possibility to build coalitions, to find ways to represent everyone.

As I was traveling the country attending protests and doing interviews, I thought about this constantly. I interviewed progressive Democrats in Alabama, Arkansas, Idaho. Where was their representation on the federal level? In Idaho, what of the 33 percent of voters who voted for Joe Biden—outside of politics, 33 percent is a big percentage! And what of Texas, where 5.8 million people voted for Trump, but 5.2 million voted for Biden? Or California, where 6 million voters selected Trump? This lack of representation is compounded by the fact that we frequently elect presidents who don't win the popular votes.

As someone who spent 15 years teaching, I also think of it this way. If I had a class of 30 students, and ten of those students were never present, disengaged, and ultimately failed my class, I'd lose my job. And yet, we create political systems with no incentive to enfranchise the "losing" side. We've created a system where good faith is assumed, but our institutions don't demand or enforce it, so are easily overwhelmed by bad faith (in the way that Sartre talks about it) actors.

As the razor-thin decisions came back across the country after the 2022 midterms. Multiple races were decided by less than a percentage point—a sharply divided citizenry. Deciding that half of the country does not have a voice will continue to create conditions where the disenfranchised look outside of the system for validation. We need to do better.

I vividly remember watching the 2000 Bush v. Gore returns. My brother Ben (the one who got pepper-sprayed later, protesting Silent Sam) was nine at the time, and had homework to watch the election returns and color a map: red for states called for Bush, blue for states called for Gore. But Ben, who had listened to family conversations about the Green Party, brought out a green crayon and lined it up next to its red and blue friends, and got sadder and sadder as the map became red and blue with nary a state called for Nader.

At some point, confident that Gore had it in the bag, I drifted out to watch the election returns with my friends. We drank. "Florida, Florida, Florida" Tim Russert wrote on a whiteboard, predicting the centrality of that race in deciding the course of our nation's history. (Of course, little did we know that the Supreme Court would step in to stop the recount in Florida, essentially declaring Bush president.)

2. Envision a robust democracy

I see a real possibility for the failure of American democracy, and the end of the Constitution as a genuine governing document. Too many tinpot dictatorships have lovely constitutions that are completely ignored.

—AN ORGANIZER FROM THE DEEP SOUTH, 2020

After the confounding results of the 2022 midterms, where Democrats managed to gain seats in the Senate, narrowly lose the House, and gain governors seats, legal genius Sherrilyn Ifill warned against complacency: "the Democrats were saved, not democracy." This was eerily reminiscent of a conversation I had with one protester from San Francisco shortly before the 2018 midterms who said: "I'm optimistic that Democrats will win the midterms. But I'm pessimistic about the future of democracy in this country." We've been able to stave off existential threats to democracy using the Democratic Party as a tool, but we've been less successful at creating a nationwide movement for democracy.

If you are trying to shore up a backsliding country, what should you do? When a democracy is backsliding, how can protests reassert a hold on democracy? How can protesters articulate a cultural, normative vision of democracy, not just demand procedural improvements? There must be a focus not just on the strategic or behavioral level of activism, but also on the ethos and the identity articulated by activists. This is key—both to understanding the possibilities and limits of American protest, as well as to creating a blueprint for democratic salvation in the years to come.

One of the prevalent questions that activists reflected on was whether it was possible to save the US version of democracy, or if it would need to be burned down and rebuilt (or, indeed, if that was what was already happening). As one organizer mused: "We're coming up on the 250th anniversary of the United States. I'm hoping we can start afresh. We won't be the country that we were. If you look at every other democracy, they've had to start several times. We're the only ones that didn't." One activist put more succinctly: "The racism is so deep in this country, and the police are so out of control, it feels like all we can do is burn it all down and rebuild."

Reimagining a new world is not only about institutions: it's about imagining how we treat every member of our society. Elena, who you'll meet in Dispatches from the Field 6, believes that the pursuit of happiness is individual, but dignity is a communal pursuit:

> Re-imagine a new democracy that is actually written and built on the principle that everyone has the right to dignity. That's very different than the right to pursue happiness, right? The right to pursue happiness is very individualistic and the right to dignity is something that we all must play a part in. It has a very different kind of contract. The reckoning on racial justice is the start of a massive cultural change that needs to happen in order for this country to survive in any comfortable way. But it means that people will have to be uncomfortable for a long time.

Creating and then holding space for that discomfort is a central part of what we need to do to achieve real change. No one is immune from the fact that this is a precarious moment for democracy, and that exciting and unpredictable things can happen. This was palpable in my interviews. As Perla, who you met in Dispatches from the Field 5, said in our final conversation in 2020:

"Power is shifting back to the people, and nothing makes me want to work harder than to make sure that continues to happen. I really feel like we're on the precipice of a big change if we're able to keep our democracy at all."[7]

3. F**k the patriarchy

We can't possibly hope to preserve and grow our democracy without, in the immortal words a long and illustrious line of women, "fuck the patriarchy." "Grab 'em by the pussy" wasn't enough to keep more than half of the White women in this country from voting for Trump.

I know that you know, but let's get into the weeds for a minute anyway. Let's start with reproductive freedom and bodily autonomy. I remember how my body felt in 2021 when the *Dobbs* decision leaked. Even before then, it was clear that red states no longer felt beholden to follow laws that no longer served their interest. Texas, and then Mississippi, passed abortion bans that were prohibited by *Roe v. Wade*—which didn't end up mattering, of course. Now let's be clear: all of the pageantry, the denial of a seat for Merrick Garland, the appointment of Amy Coney Barrett to desecrate the seat that RBG held for too long—all of that was a set up to put the women of this country in their places.

In case you need a tangible reminder of what this looked like, remember back to the 2017 confirmation of Jeff Sessions as attorney general. Then Majority Leader Mitch McConnell silenced Senator Elizabeth Warren when spoke in objection of Sessions confirmation because of his abhorrent record on civil rights. McConnell said: "Senator Warren was giving a lengthy speech. She had appeared to violate the rule. She was warned. She was given an explanation. **Nevertheless, she persisted.**" This became a rallying call for women breaking barriers and fighting against the persistent political misogyny of the time. (My husband has it on a t-shirt!)

Before *Dobbs*, when Texas started to pass its anti-choice bills, my family and I were at a crossroads about where we wanted to live next.

We'd left Nebraska and were torn—Austin or Brooklyn. Jim had job prospects in both places. We had family and very close friends in both places. What decided it for us, then, was the abortion situation.[8] We didn't want to raise our girls somewhere that they would be second-class citizens, we didn't want to raise our son somewhere that he witnessed, every day, girls and women being treated that way. Our money, our labor, our community was better spent somewhere that had its problems, for sure, but we were not worried that our kids could go to jail for giving a friend an abortion pill.[9]

Since then, there's been a political back-and-forth that makes clear that this issue matters (look at the special elections and ballot initiatives from Kansas to Wisconsin to Kentucky that have been decided with abortion as a main issue). Look, too, at the laws—in Texas and Idaho and Alabama—that are being passed on state and local levels to restrict a woman's right to travel to receive abortion care (and it's being done like pieces on a Risk board, blocking off travel—like through Mitchell County, Texas, which lies between Dallas and New Mexico).

Lest we wonder if this is only about controlling the bodies of people who can get pregnant, let's consider the state of life for families with kids under the patriarchy. As I write, in 2023, the child tax credit expired. Childcare where I live is about $2,000 a month during the year and about $3,000 a month during the summer (PER CHILD). We're last, or among the last, in the world for paid parental leave, guaranteed sick leave, universal health care, affordable college—all of the things that make parents feel like parenting is something they can do.

Obviously, the authoritarianism of the patriarchy goes beyond parenting (although I believe reproductive freedom is at the core of it). They want to ban drag shows. It's easier for Barack Hussain Obama to be elected than Hillary Clinton (or Kamala Harris . . .). There are currently 25 women in the US Senate—at 25 percent this is the most women that have ever served, and 42 percent of women who have ever served. It's bleak out there.

RAINN (Rape, Abuse & Incest National Network) tells us that, out of every 1,000 sexual assaults, 975 perpetrators will walk free, in a country where over half of women and one in three men experience sexual violence in their lifetimes. Women earn less than men over the course of their lifetimes, with women of color earning much less.

We know, we know, we know, and yet we get locked into a situation where nothing policy-wise ever changes.

For so many years, I screamed into the void about how bloody hard it was to work with young children when the math never added up. And then, midway through the pandemic, I took my toys and went home. Decided to do things my way, even if it was going to be hard (which it is). I don't have to give my labor to people who devalue it.

4. F**k White supremacy

We need to talk about the costs of Whiteness. In a gorgeous, moving narrative simply entitled #Black Lives Matter, Bahar Davary recounts the day that she learned of George Zimmerman's acquittal in the death of Trayvon Martin. She gives her students this assignment:

> 'Between the years of 1885 and 1908, policies of Leopold II caused the death of at least 10–15 million Congolese. Why do history textbooks say nothing, or next to nothing, about it?' Students listened closely, as she continued: 'What is the relation between this bloody event, its erasure from history books, and the movements of Malcolm and Martin? And finally: Do you have hope that what James Baldwin declared fifty years ago as the perpetual achievement of the impossible in his book *The Fire Next Time* (1963), to become a possibility in the twenty-first century? For those who may not remember, Baldwin had tied the possibility for a real change for Black people in this country to radical changes in the American political and social structure.' The class fell silent, as she sat down and buried

her face in a book, with a disquiet feeling of trepidation
and hope.

People who have been marginalized often contribute to the public
good in good faith, and then wind up consistently at the bottom of
constantly reshuffled social stratifications.[10] How do you stop that
from happening? Politicians take Black and Brown votes for granted,
without giving access to power (or to the privileges of the state). This
involves a reversal of what Juliet Hooker terms the "democratic sacrifice" required of Black citizens and building an actual multiracial
democracy where people bear equally the "burden of citizenship." Who
is democracy for?

As James Baldwin writes in 1963, absent reconciliation and trans-
formation, the knowing of the crimes against Black people in this country does not repair the original sin—the belief that "that the authors of
devastation should also be innocent. It is the innocence which consti-
tutes the crime." Of course, this is what is going on across red states in
this country, as entire school curricula are being rewritten to avoid any
risk of kids feeling "guilty" about our country's racial history. This is
another way of rendering them "innocent," of removing the historical
legacy of privilege. Of making it so that kids no longer can learn in
school that we inherit our place in society from decisions made in the
past—that we are not here because someone worked hard or someone
else got lucky, but rather because there are structural events that shaped
who could work, *who* could get lucky.

And without understanding our past, we have no hope to
understand the present. As Brittany Packnett Cunningham tweeted
after a murderous racist tried to shoot up an Historically Black College,
got turned away, and so killed three Black people in a Dollar General
instead: "A white gunman just killed 3 Black grocery shoppers in a state
that won't let children learn why" (@mspackyetti, August 26, 2023).
This is dangerous—if we allow both the content and function of multiracial democracy to disappear from our schools, I worry about our

ability to get it back. I mostly believe that knowledge finds a way to make itself free, but I have my moments where I believe that this rewriting of history might succeed.

We also need to be wary of the way that racism and permission structures surrounding White supremacy affect our own thinking; as one White activist told me: "There's rising fascism in our own communities, in our own places. I even notice it in myself sometimes. The part of my brain that was trained to be racist from a young age feels more excited to tell me more racist thoughts more of the time. Racism is around everywhere in a deeper way than it was." Trump gave permission for jokes that were told behind closed doors to come into the open. One way you can change the world? Withdraw permission for your racist cousin to be racist. Tell them to explain the joke. Make the room uncomfortable.

5. F**k unchecked capitalism

You probably know people who say things like "I'm economically conservative but socially liberal," which tends to be code for "maybe Republicans will cut my taxes too." Truly, economic and social policy are inseparable. You cannot be economically conservative and socially liberal, because of the deep extent to which your economic decisions affect the social world that we build together.[11]

Mike Johnson, the theocrat who was elected as the Republican's *fifth* choice for Speaker of the House in 2023, is quoted by CBS News as saying that *Roe v. Wade* "gave constitutional cover to the elected killing of unborn children in America, period. You think about the implications of that on the economy. We're all struggling here to cover the bases of social security and Medicare and Medicaid and all the rest. If we had all those able-bodied workers in the economy, we wouldn't be going upside down and toppling over like this." In other words, women should be forced to have babies so those babies can pay taxes.

These two examples, put together, show us the extent to which economics (cost of living, wages) drives our social world—and of course what capitalists and Republicans are willing to trade in exchange for not paying taxes. Bodily autonomy, secure housing, access to health care.

Of course, Bernie Sanders and Elizabeth Warren did great things to put economic justice in the national conversation. And there is real evidence that union organizing is having a transformative effect on how we do business in America. For the first time in the nation's history, Joe Biden marched with strikers in Detroit during the massive automotive industry strike. And it worked; consider the labor victories just from 2023: Teamsters and UPS. Health care workers. Hollywood writers. UAW. Starbucks. The list goes on: when we organize, we win.

6. Tell a story about this vision of democracy

To articulate a vision of democracy, you need people to understand the fundamental tenets of why democracy is good. Right now, our overly technocratic articulation of government in civics classes does no one any favors.

Even kids can understand the need to talk about a better world, and civics instruction in our country badly does them a disservice, focusing on the institutions and procedures without the vital details that make democracy something worth fighting for.[12] Why do we try to explain how we elect representatives before we explain what a democracy is and why everyone should choose how we live together? It's like teaching kids the alphabet and phonics devoid of any content (looking at you, NYC), and then expecting them to be brilliant authors. We need to teach a love of democracy, a protectiveness of citizenship, before we teach the particulars of a given system of government. Why does the number of Supreme Court justices matter more than a discussion of how we need to resolve disputes as a country and have systems to do that?

Because of the utterly anemic way that citizenship and civics are taught in this country, for the most part, we are left with a situation where no one can engage in a vigorous defense of democracy or democratic principles. And there are powerful groups across the country acting to *remove* active learning—project-based, experiential explorations of democracy—from the way states teach civics. [📢] We can change that. But first, as we learn in *The Little Prince*, we have to teach people to love democracy: "If you want to build a ship, don't drum up people to collect wood and don't assign them tasks and work, but teach them to long for the endless immensity of the sea."

How do we understand building a future for our country? What does that look like, beyond ideals like "equity" and "justice" and "freedom" and "opportunity"? Maybe we can get closer to policies "reproductive freedoms" and "reparations for slavery" and "redistribution of wealth" or "abolition" or "abolition of billionaires." But even then, what are the structures, institutions, cultural shifts that have to happen to work toward these outcomes? Can our current democracy produce some of these? If not what needs to change?

As I sat down to write this book, the George Floyd protests faded, leading to reactionary protests by Republicans against reading and library books at the CRT boogeyman; Biden was elected, COVID lingered despite vaccines, and the question remained: What next? What models can future protesters use and imagine?

One of the activists I interviewed worked for Valarie Kaur (who, full disclosure, is a good friend of my brother's from law school). We talked about her book *Revolutionary Love*, which espouses a cultural and social shift toward a politics based on love.[13] As we build community, we envision one where love—sometimes a fierce type of love—makes space for change.

And this matters in particular because right-wing governments do not operate on love. They operate on hate and mistrust. They ruin countries by forcing people into entrenched identity groups instead of finding ways to bring people back together. And, this kind of socially constructed mistrust, can be awfully hard to recover from.[14]

7. Rechart your relationship with the Democratic Party

In the next two sections, I make the case for reenvisioning the relationship between yourself and the Democratic Party. Parties lock you into a system—make you buy into this system that isn't working. We should have sway over the system, but put pressure on it not just to adopt our issue stances, but also to be willing to take chances on our candidates.

Democrats—you have to do better by your activist allies. More radical protesters were uncomfortable with the shift from progressive politics to a "vote blue no matter who" philosophy. "It's sort of awkward," one organizer said, "once the election came it was 'okay let's just get as many Democrats elected as possible no matter who they are basically.'"

The relationship between the Democratic Party and activists has evolved in strange, often contradictory ways over the past decade: One midwestern activist told me: "we're rogue, and we are at war with the Democratic Party in the city. We don't care about them anymore and they don't care about us, and we just win over them . . ." Her organization chose to exclusively endorse Working Family candidates over the more moderate Democrats who were endorsed by "the machine." (In New York, you can also vote for Democratic candidates on the Working Families ticket.)

In addition to using resistance groups as a backdrop at rallies, there was also a sense that organizers were being used for labor, but without the ability to shape strategy: "The Democratic Party told us they wanted to bring the group leaders in and listen to us, but in the end all they really asked was to turn out volunteers to door knock. There's not much reciprocation in supporting the work of the post-election groups." Here again was an echo of the way that leaders of more marginalized communities talked about the post-election groups. Additionally, longstanding civic groups described a tone-deaf approach taken by the Democratic Party in their state: " We left the Democrats pretty early on because they were using sort of a cookbook approach to outreach to voters, and we didn't think it was effective." As one person organizing Milwaukee quipped, "All of their material was geared at Wisconsin dairy farmers, not people in the city working three jobs."[15] This of course resonates with the critique that the Democratic Party was out of touch with working-class Americans (not to mention the utterly awful, end-of-history texts and emails they send). We need tell stories about democracy and why it's worth saving all the time, not just in the lead up to elections.

8. Challenge your theory of change

We need to engage in political struggle regardless of who is elected. We need to be strategic enough to stay engaged even as we push politicians to the left. Social movements often disarm and demobilize because of electoral success—even when it's not paired with issue success. For example, Heaney and Rojas show how there was a total collapse of the anti-war movement after the 2006 elections, after the Democrats took control over the House: "It was no longer 'necessary' to have an anti-war movement in the streets because the Democratic Party was the anti-war movement. Starting in 2007, a democratically controlled Congress could use the power of the purse to defund the Iraq War and force President Bush slowly to withdraw US forces."[16] But—here's the punchline—they didn't. We didn't withdraw from the war in Iraq; in fact, Obama even used drones to assassinate people, including killing a US citizen with a drone strike in Yemen.

This is a telling moment in the Obama presidency, because he was forced to confront the fact that he's out of line with many in his party. As Obama told Jonathan Chait in a 2016 interview: "I mean this sincerely: I'm glad the left pushes me on this. I've said to my staff and I've said to my joint chiefs, I've said in the Situation Room: I don't ever want to get to the point where we're that comfortable with killing." This quotation embodies the frustration that the left had with Obama—an acknowledgement that he understood their position, but a refusal to give organizers or movements any real credit for setting the agenda or moving the needle on the issue. At the end of this interview with Jonathan Chait in 2016, Obama reflects on his decision-making: "What I've tried to do is to move the needle in the right direction, to set some trends in the right direction. But there's gonna be a lot more work to do."

A question at the core of this book and any book that talks about democracy or politics or culture: How does power work? I'm not sure we have a very good working theory of power in the US.[17] We have one story that tells us we're the most polarized we've ever been as a country. We have another story that tells us that we're at an inflection point where we keep, as an electorate, changing up who holds the power, changing the political parties of our representatives. We have another story that is an end-of-history narrative where Republicans have won, they outplayed us on the local level by paying attention to school boards and on the national level by Federalist Society-ing our way to a generation of conservative judges, and another story where progressives have won the battle for hearts and minds, and we know this because a Republican presidential candidate has won the popular vote only once in 30 years (and that was in 2004).

We have the bananagrams "woke mind virus" that the right claims has affected everything from the Chairman of the Joint Chiefs of Staff to all education including math textbooks. To the point where we're seriously entertaining the claim that there were bright spots to slavery.

It seems obvious to me that the total meltdown of Republicans across the country, banning abortion, defunding Diversity, Equity, and Inclusion (DEI) programs, forbidding the teaching of race—all of this is a pretty good indication that something from these movements touched a live nerve.

What does this have to do with power, who has it, and how they wield and protect it? Well, Michel Foucault, a French social theorist who talks a lot about power, talks about social control this way: We used to exercise power from institutions that would then wield power over people. The state would discipline, punish, execute people in public. We'd lock people (women especially) in mental institutions. Schools would be heavy-handed in their imposition of discipline and demand for order.

Over time, power becomes more insidious: We begin to police ourselves, and each other, so the state could maintain control without having to act. Right now, the state is showing its hand again. The SCOTUS, and the Republican leadership, they know they've lost the power for subtle control, and so they are trying everything they can to amass power. We know that their goal is to end the right to fair and free elections, to instill power by fear and division.

Because Republicans have decided that their best bet is to overtly undermine democracy, then you consolidate power, that makes it visible—and thus easier to resist.

Which means we got this. Not that it's easy, not that it's in the bag, but that we can see the face and shape of the enemy, which means we know what we're up against.

I thought that the most refreshing part of the past ten years was when people started saying the quiet part out loud because that leveled the playing field. When Uncle Morris, whose "off-color jokes" were always "behind doors among friends," realized it was safe to be racist in public, that was a step in the right direction—because it saves us the trouble of hunting those racists down. We can identify them. And when the Hitler-loving folks started feeling like it was safe to be in the wild again, it meant that the time for gaslighting was over. Bring it into the light so we can fucking confront and fix it.

You don't need to organize, you don't need to attend protests, but you do need to realize that being apolitical is a political choice. Democracy is about protecting each other and our chosen community.

Even if you don't want to attend a single thing, you need to learn how to make a loud, clear articulation in support of democracy. The pragmatism of Indivisible, was successful at pushing Congress left, needs to be paired with multigenerational struggles.

If you haven't seen the movie *Goodbye, Lenin,* you should—it's a hysterically funny account of life in East Germany during the fall of the Berlin Wall (even my students thought it was funny, so you know that it's true). In the movie, the mother, who is a staunch supporter of the communist government, takes her right to file citizen petitions (Eingaben) very seriously. These petitions were a way for East German citizens living in a highly regulated society to express their displeasure with the state (without, for example, the opportunity to participate in free and fair elections)—and supporters of the regime took their right to petition to heart (Betts and Betts 2010). Indeed, Václav Havel circulated a petition in 1989 entitled "A Few Questions," which is credited with helping to bring about the fall of the Communist Party.

This kind of use of voice is illustrated by a concept game theorists call exit, voice, loyalty. When people are in opposition to their government, they can do three things: they can move to another country, they can stop voting, they can move to a commune and live off the grid (these are all "exit"). They can shut up and be good citizens and soldiers and act the part anyway (this is "loyalty"). Or they can decide neither is a good option—they can say "not in our name" and voice their displeasure. This is why we fight: because we *can* keep using our voice. We can complicate the narrative.

An oppositional consciousness means we're doing this all the time, not because we want to burn it all down (although we do want to burn some things down) but because we care enough to want to keep building.

9. Maybe you should run for office

If we agree that we need to work within and outside of the system, it's clear to me that we need to flood the zone with progressive people running for office. There are real barriers to overcome for young people, people of color, far-left people, people with disabilities, who want to find their way into politics. If you're reading this and wondering "should I run?"—consider this your ask and reassurance. Yes, you should run for office! What do you want to run for? How can we help? (No, really—there are a dozen, at least, awesome organizations out there trying to build a deep bench of progressive candidates, from the efforts of Moms Demand Action to elect gun-sense candidates to EMILY's List electing pro-choice women to Run for Something which is trying to recruit young voters. Run for office!)

I talked to a lot of women who considered running for office for the first time based on their experience running Indivisible chapters. For some, organizing gave them a way to build relationships with progressive political candidates, and they became their staff.

A woman associated with Indivisible who ran for office, and then ended her primary early, reflected on her experience: "I was not prepared for how nasty a campaign could get. It's difficult for someone who has been a committed activist for many years to become a politician. The thing that I worried about is: I'll have to give up my activism. I don't want to have to modify my words or my actions based on, okay, should I be seen at this rally? Is that going to play in my moderate district? Running for office is a lifetime goal, but it's probably not for me."

Although the midterms proved to be spectacularly successful for female candidates, there was some concern over their ability to face the difficulties of campaigning. One female activist mused: "I worry that first-time female candidates are going to break on the rocks of inexperience." Many of them evoked the anger they felt over Clinton's treatment, saying they felt this anger on the local level too—women were expected to be both soft and feminine and politicians were expected to be tough and decisive, creating a dichotomy difficult to navigate. Not all felt this way—one retired man living in the South said that he was so excited about how empowered women were, and he felt like local elections were really providing an exciting avenue for women.

Running for office is also a way to make sure that your community reflects the values that are meaningful to you. My friend Wendy ran for school board, and won, against a slate of Moms for Liberty Candidates in 2023. Lucy McBath ran for Congress, and won her election, after her son Jordan was shot and killed.[18] Sometimes you can make change from within, and running for office is the way to do that.

10. Stop eating our own

The next two sections think about how to construct a big tent movement that is still true to our values. This is so hard, because by virtue of having a big tent, we don't have a firm identity and label that we unite behind. People on the right *love* MAGA so much that there's now a whole brand associated with it (MAGA rap, anyone?).[19] There are particular structures that endorse this—charismatic authoritarian corners of the internet in particular. Not so for us (though Obama Girl tried to make it happen).[20] Sara, one of my early readers and best friends, who has been active in the pro-choice and antiracist protests in New York, grumbled to me: "I hate the word liberal, I hate the label progressive, I hate being called an activist." Even though she acknowledged that she is all of those things, by default if nothing else, but finds the labels to be constricting.

From the Bernie and Hillary wars to debates over how much support to give Biden as a candidate and then as president, there are real divides in terms of how progressive the movement needed to be. The progressive wing of the Democratic Party, and the Democratic Socialists of America (DSA) tried to push the party to the left, arguing (rightly) that there is no reason to believe that Republicans will go soft on people in the middle—and there's evidence that they've won.

Interestingly, the General Social Survey shows us that, 50 years ago, 44 percent of Republicans identified as conservative—now it's 73 percent. In the same time period, Democrats have gone from 34 percent to 61 percent identifying as liberal Democrats—but almost all of that movement has been since 2016.

In the interviews I did, there was often a feeling of defeat, and a sense that the left was willing to eat their own and participate in purity contests. In one call, a longtime organizer sounded particularly down. I asked her why, and she told me: "Right now, you've hit me at a bit of a bad time, because I'm kind of depressed that sometimes as progressives, we eat our own." Another more moderate activist reflected the same worries: "The left is waging war—they call themselves progressives, but they are punching at the middle, at centrist Democrats and establishment Democrats, and meanwhile the Republican Party is stealing SCOTUS seats and stacking the judiciary."[21] [📢] From this way of thinking, making real attempts to bring together the different wings of progressivism was key to making any real change. Indeed, the threat felt existential. However correct this call is—and I do think that there's real value in coming up with a united front against fascism that sees a role for all in the movement—a necessary part of that is that people are willing to give up and confront their privileges, which brings us to . . .

11. Calling people in, not out

People are better than their governments, and better than the systems and institutions that govern them. People can change, learn, develop empathy. When you talk about change, there's often the sense that the previous generation (the "old left") had their chance, and that this moment requires new ideas and new ways of organizing. As one activist lamented, we "need new people with new ideas or we'll die—something that the old left doesn't understand." And of course this is true. However, we can't afford to dismiss as irrelevant everyone who does not fit the latest rendition of "woke." As organizers Kelly Hayes and Mariame Kaba write: "White supremacy and classism have forced many wedges between our communities. Great harms have been committed and very difficult conversations are needed, but refusing to do that work, in this historical moment, is an abdication of responsibility. It is no exaggeration to say that the whole world is at stake, and we cannot afford to minimize what that demands of us."[22]

And this work of building a civic identity, an identity not just as a private citizen but as someone invested in democracy, is critical to crafting a future. One activist said:

> Demographics is absolutely fucking not destiny if we aren't talking to people and giving them a political ethos and engaging them and having them build their identities as voters, as civically engaged, civically minded people. We don't give people a sense of what it means to being in a community, then we will lose. Organization is built on the sense we don't just come in when we want people to vote for our candidates. We engage them and build organization so they can become part of the fabric, a social fabric, and feel a social duty and responsibility to protect that community.

This brilliant quote underscores all of the important points in organizing: giving people a political ethos, creating a community, and then charging people to protect that community. How can discrete acts of protest transform into what Mansbridge and others call oppositional consciousness with the capacity to change the country's culture?

12. Take leadership from young people

Speaking from 2024, I ask you: How did we wind up in a situation where two consecutive presidential election cycles were dominated by White men who were born in the 1940s? Why did both Ruth

Bader Ginsberg (RBG) and Dianne Feinstein die in office, rather than allowing a younger person to take their place (if RBG had retired during Obama's term, would we still have Roe?).[23] Although a lot of people immediately think of term limits when they're faced with these questions, I think it's also a matter of social trust: how can you trust your children enough so that you can retire, so that you can hand them the world?[24]

What is true in electoral politics is also true in movement spaces. Part of our future depends on letting young people organize. Delaney Tarr, one of the survivors of the Parkland shooting who organized the March For Our Lives rallies after, wrote a great *Teen Vogue* article in December 2022 about how we shouldn't wait for the kids to save us—but of course in many ways we're doing exactly that. One of my awesome students said, "I do art—it's not like I'm helping society." Of course, there is no society without art. We need art as a form of protest, but we also are protesting so there is space to do art. They need each other.

Tanisha has faith that young people will be able to save us: "The young people who organize are the same age as the founding fathers, except for Ben Franklin who was an old man. I feel in good hands. I love 'em to death. I also think they have the tenacity to stay in the streets . . . I love that they stay in the streets. I love that they're demanding police out of their schools. I love it. And I tell elders: 'stand back stand down and let them go.'" Of course, we should always be ready to save ourselves. But this new generation—they're incredible.

13. Finally, find and replace what drains your energy

This book emphasizes slow approaches to organizing because, although parts of politics will always *drain* energy stores, hopefully other parts will replenish them. It's hard to resist, but it is easier to nurture—to affirmatively work toward a future we want.

In this book, I badly wanted to move away from things that would drain the energy of the reader. This meant, literally, doing a "find and replace," for two words. The first was the word Trump—everywhere I could omit his name, I did. We're building forward. The second find and replace was for "hard." As one early reader said, "Yeah, it's hard, but so is going to the gym." Acknowledging that it's hard shouldn't be the end—it should be foundational, and then allow growth from there.

DISPATCHES FROM THE FIELD 4:
MEET GEORGIE

Georgie is a socialist organizer from the Northwest. Here is her story:

> I lived in Florida from 1979 to 1989 and got exposed to feminist thinking through some of my studies. So, while I was in Florida, I think I actually went to a couple of national organizations of women groups and nothing but an old bunch of old biddies who were not interested in some young newbie coming in with lots of energy. When I was deciding it was time to leave Florida I just kind of made a commitment to myself that it was time to get involved politically and start fighting more for women's rights. When I got here and was finishing my internship for my master's degree, I got involved with a pro-choice group which was basically kind of like having meetings to talk about what they were going to have at the next meeting, which I found really annoying and so started pushing it forward and they ended up hiring me part-time to run a phone bank to do voter I.D. for a Democratic candidate running against a really anti-choice candidate.

I realized that doing political work and activism was my niche that I was looking for where I felt the most comfortable and being a very strong loudmouth female who was not afraid to speak up and didn't care if I got a ration of shit for doing so, it fit my personality quite well. I worked for a political group for three and a half years and unfortunately part of the reason it went defunct was lack of funding. Money became a problem. I worked at one of the special sessions in Montana and then I worked for the state for a year as a case manager for adults with developmental disabilities, which I have to say was during the legislative session, and so I recruited some of my high-functioning clients to go testify when they were going to cut the side of ones that can cut the budget for developmental disability services, and took them to a hearing where I got them to speak out where the governor was there and the head of the agency. Not only did they not cut the budget, they actually increased it.

Then I had met my husband who is now my ex-husband: he was one of the candidates that we had endorsed. After that, I went back to school to get a second master's with the thought of working toward a Ph.D. in sociology, but I have since had to have four back surgeries and that just put the kibosh on work. So, I am now disabled but I make organic soaps and lotions and sell at farmer's markets and then do a lot of political organizing and work with the local chapter of the Democratic Socialists for America.

FIND YOUR PEOPLE—AND THEN FIND THEIR PEOPLE

Although my family wasn't particularly active in politics when I was young, I knew that protesting was in my veins. My dad burned his draft card and hitchhiked across the country. One of my earliest memories is of my dad telling a creepy story about finding a graveyard in Vermont so they could help a buddy dodge the draft (even as my Uncle David, his older brother and best friend, enlisted and went to war). I grew up on stories of my mom wearing me on her back to an anti-nuclear rally in Central Park in the early 1980s. This spirit of rebelliousness, and a love of protest stories, has always been with me. In high school and college, I surrounded myself with activists: I was never quite one of the cool kids, but cool-kid adjacent, waiting to see what would happen next.

I also was a junkie for books written by the Beats in the 1950s and 1960s. In *On the Road*, Jack Kerouac says: "The only people that interest me are the mad ones, the ones who are mad to live, mad to talk, desirous of everything at the same time, the ones that never yearn or say a commonplace thing . . . but burn, burn, burn like Roman candles across the night." My favorite part of the quote is this next part: "and I shambled after as usual as I've been doing all my life after people that interest me, because the only people that interest me are the mad ones, the ones who are mad to live, mad to talk, mad to be saved, desirous of everything at the same time." I love this, love the verb shambled. After the 2016 election, I didn't know how to organize to save the world, but I knew how to shamble after the people who did, listen to their stories, and then write this book to share them with the world. This was my "why," my way to make sense out of the chaos of this world.

So . . . how do we make this democratic awakening happen? This chapter is all about how to find your "why" for getting involved in the quest to save democracy, and how to find the people you want to make change with along the way. We can't rely on political parties to democratize for us—we need to claim and reform our democracy ourselves. I don't mean reading the news, talking about politics, voting, or even registering people to vote, even though that's part of it—and an important part. As Joe Katz wrote after the 2023 midterms on Bluesky, "No, electoralism won't save us. Yes, it is in fact a necessary part of the toolkit of forcing change. And ceding it to people you disagree with is ridiculously counterproductive" (@joekatz45, November 7, 2023). Think of the chess game. Think back to the map Lara Trump shared—visual electionist propaganda is part of the MAGA strategy, a way to spread weakness and sow doubt. There's no question we need to vote, and not cede the powers and resources of the system to fascists. And we also need to sustain an *oppositional consciousness,* being constantly suspicious of threats to democracy, and having a toolkit to neutralize or push back against those threats (that's Step One). Once we do, here's the second step—find your why, find your people, and start creating or joining in the movement to save democracy.

No one can do this work alone: the work we do is in solidarity with each other, with our community (whether a physical or virtual community); finding your "why" is tied up with finding who your people are: these are one and the same project. It's lonely to struggle alone for a better world.

DISPATCHES FROM THE FIELD 5:
MEET PERLA

Perla, a middle-aged founder of a phenomenally successful Indivisible chapter in the southwest, knew she had to be in DC for the Women's March in 2017. Here's her story:

> It was something I'll never forget. I had a stopover in Dallas. I was wearing my pink hat and I saw other women in the Dallas airport at the gate for the flight to DC wearing pink hats and I knew that we were all going to the march. A few of us, I think probably six or seven of us, had on the pink pussy hat and kind of just chuckled and giggled. And then as other people in the boarding area saw us beginning to talk, other random people just started coming over because we had the hats on, so they knew we were going. Pretty soon we had 40 or 50 people in the little group going, "Oh my God, we're going to DC," just getting really excited. On the plane, I asked the flight attendant to ask everybody going to the Women's March to raise their hand. She took a photograph of that on my phone, and it wound up on national TV, because it was this flight full of people that didn't know each other and 80 percent of the people on that plane, their hands were in the air to go to the march in DC. It was quite remarkable. Then at the march, it was so crowded. There were so many more people than they ever expected. I never got close to the stage. I never heard a speaker. I didn't even hear the music play. I lost my group. Couldn't get to the bathroom and I didn't care about any of it. It was tremendous.

Do this . . .

Each of the next three chapters is organized around ideas of things you can do, and what to keep in mind as you do them. As you begin to find your reason for protesting, there are four more things you should do:

- Know your why.
- Find your people (and make sure they can participate).
- Tell your story.
- Learn the history of resistance.

Know Your Why

If you want to change the world, you need a "why": a reason that you're going to engage in activism instead of doing literally anything else. Most likely, you have a series of reasons why, short-term and long-term, instrumental and ethical. Here's my advice: write a list of reasons, and revisit them often, like a mission statement. For me, it's an ongoing list of things that I'm mad about that I keep in the notes app on my phone. Whenever I get too apathetic, I figure that there's no need for this book because the good guys will win, I take a peek at that list and get fired up again.

Finding your why might be harder now, with so many different issues vying for attention *and* when there isn't necessarily a crisis propelling you forward (besides the crazy headlines every day that are hurling us toward the wholesale disavowal of democracy). One activist who had been active in the 1960s told me that Walter Cronkite's chronicling of the Vietnam War built a "crescendo of dissatisfaction," leading to massive anti-war demonstrations. [📢] In the 1980s, she was friends with people who were part of ACT UP; [📢] they knew that if they didn't speak out and get the government to care, they would die of AIDS. The threat was existential.

Today, the narrative is more fractured—there's an issue a day and you're always playing catch up. This can lead to burnout unless you can find your why as a way to guide you through the process.

Take a minute and make your list. Here's mine: I'm fighting because we're doing this shit again, that the country is so fractured that, as you're reading this, Trump might be president. I'm fighting because my dear friends have a trans daughter and are so scared of a Republican presidency that they're working on European citizenship. It's for women who are going septic all over this country carrying babies that have no chance of survival because of these abortion bans. It's because daycare costs $2,000 a month and student loan payments are restarting. And it's because the richest countries on Earth have decided that letting migrants drown is the best immigration policy we can muster. There's a lot to be mad about—a lot of reasons to stay in the game.

It's important to "right-size" these goals: if your reasons are too specific, you're going to accomplish a goal and then run out of steam (this is why governments so often try to accommodate protesters—pacify them with little wins so they don't go after the big wins). If your goals, on the other hand, are too abstract, then it's easy to get frustrated with never accomplishing anything. (Dismantling capitalism is a great goal, but what are small steps to getting there?)

Election cycles and media narratives are built against slow organizing. (It's 11 am and I've gotten ten emails about how I need to donate *now* to defeat Trump and save the Democratic Party—fast money is the name of the game.) The insistence on the horse race, the idea that every election is the most important election of our lives, makes it hard to slow down. To sit out an election cycle to focus on something big. To decide what needs your time and talent, and put your energy there. To decide who needs your money, consider organizers instead of candidates. They'll be in the field regardless of who wins a primary.

Find Your People (and Make Sure They Can Participate)

To do this work, to feel like you're not screaming into the void, you need to find your people—and then start networking out, finding the broader community of allies. Coalition building is complicated—who do you want to ally with? Why? What will the coalition look like? Part of thinking about allyship strategically is recognizing that we need an umbrella of liberation to tap into the identity and community building—a type of coalitional politics. We might not be singing the same song, but it would be helpful if we were at least listening to the same Spotify playlist (go listen to "Paper Rings" on Step Two's playlist right now and then come back. I'll wait).[1]

Who are the people you imagine participating in your organizing space? What are the barriers that might keep them from being able to fully commit, and how you overcome them? A universal design for organizing helps us create space for everyone. The type of people you invite to your table determines the type of organizing you do, and folks with disabilities, nonwhite folks, and folks with caring responsibilities are often excluded from the proceedings.

Once you can make your organizing space as inclusive as possible, make sure that values, resources, and actions are all in line with keeping people there. Do you need babysitters? Is there a way to compensate some folks for their labor? Is the room you meet in inclusive, and at an inclusive time? (Seven p.m. is hard for parents, especially if food/childcare isn't offered.) Who gets invited to talk? Is there an online option? What "counts" as organizing? These aren't all questions you can answer, but some of them might help you.

Tell Your Story

I have optimism in my heart. If I didn't, I would not do civil rights.

—AN ORGANIZER FROM TEXAS

Ask other people for their stories so they can become part of the fabric of activism in your community. Changing the world must be a social phenomenon—we can't do it alone. Find likeminded people who want the same thing you do. They might be online; they might be in your friend group or in your neighborhood. Charles Tilly, the great political theorist, understood that stories are perhaps the most important element in ushering through great moments of political change.[2] We know the *standard* stories, but we need *superior* ones: the Trump map is a standard story, and it's how authoritarianism makes itself concrete. It's not enough just to argue against it: we need to tell another story in its stead.

Every community has systemic organizers who have been in the game a long time—you just have to find them.[3] As one long-time activist told me: "We didn't wake up in November 2016 with this happening . . . things were building for a long time." Even if you're motivated by a very specific issue, it's helpful to understand it as part of a broader fabric of critique, resistance, and struggle. If you can find the people who were engaged before you were, and pay attention to them, you might also find that your why is deepened. In other words, you might start being mad because your kid's library is planning to ban books, and then realize that you need to put pressure on your school board before they adopt whacko civics and history standards.

You might realize that there are deep, generational racial disputes that are behind battles over where to build a park in your town.

Part of the reason that moderates don't realize there is always activism happening is because we don't tell the stories of protest. We embrace a stylized version of the civil rights movement, when in fact the entire beginning of the twentieth century was marked by turmoil and disruption. The dominant narrative of protest in the United States deemphasizes the continuous struggle that is a defining feature of our country, but particularly the early part of the twentieth century. We had anarchists! And communists! And presidential assassinations and attempted assassinations all over the place! The post-war 1950s was an all-out attempt to stay the rebelliousness of the pre-war era and to impose a set of conservative values, including anti-communist values. Of course, McCarthyism was the clearest manifestation of this. Everyone knows about the civil rights movement, at least a sanitized version of it—but all you need to do is look at Republican tweets during Black History Month to know that it's been coopted. Right around the time Twitter began flirting with its bold new identity as X, someone tweeted an AI-generated image of MLK and Donald Trump with their arms around each other, musing that if only MLK had lived he and Trump would have been best buds.

We need to retell these stories to get heroes like MLK out of their mouths (and off their feeds) and also to put as many heroic stories of activism as possible into the universe. How many activists can you name that are currently organizing? Or how many groups can you name that are doing work in your community? [📢]. If we're bad about telling stories about our history, we're even worse about celebrating the wins of the present. You need to do your resisting in public—not all the time. (The meme goes something like: "Sorry honey, I can't come to bed! Someone is wrong on the internet!") But you can tell your story of resistance, of making good trouble and being a little bit of a rabblerouser, in ways that people will want to listen.

Obama would tell these stories on the campaign trail, talking about organizing in the context of our national history; Dreir (2008) recounts this speech Obama gave: "Nothing in this country worthwhile has ever happened except when somebody somewhere was willing to hope . . . That is how workers won the right to organize against violence and intimidation. That's how women won the right to vote. That's how young people traveled South to march and to sit in and to be beaten, and some went to jail, and some died for freedom's cause."

No one tells the story that Indivisible shut down the entire GOP agenda for four years, even when they had a GOP trifecta from 2016–2018: it went in the memory vault. People roll their eyes at the Women's March, not realizing it had this unbelievably strong impact on the likelihood of people mobilizing, running for office. We should tell the story of our country as one about resistance, activism, and innovation. Practice writing the story. Pitch it to the press. Invite reporters to your new protests. Create a distinctive social media presence. But the story needs to be told, and retold. (If you don't believe me that telling stories is powerful, look at the steps that Republican-controlled legislatures across the country are taking to erase any mention of slavery or racism from our schools after Nikole Hannah-Jones told her superior story, circling back to Tilly, in the 1619 Project.)

Learn the History of Resistance

There are a few moments in my life where I've felt part of history. One of those was when I had the opportunity, in April 2018, to bring students to the Peace and Justice Summit in Montgomery, Alabama, an event hosted by Equal Justice Initiative and Bryan Stevenson to commemorate the opening of the Legacy Museum. [🔊] For two days, politicians, activists, journalists, scholars, and artists reflected on the state of racism and its history in the United States. Even as the conversation focused on the trajectory, the dark historical line, connecting lynching to mass incarceration—the conversation returned to the politics of the present, with frequent references to Barack Obama (and standing ovations for Michelle), as well as condemnations of the current administration. At one point, Michelle Alexander, engaging in a panel conversation with Sherrilyn Ifill and Jelani Cobb, remarked, "We aren't the Resistance, Trump is the resistance."[4] Her optimism that the arc of history was bending toward justice inverted the feeling of hopelessness, and of always playing defense. We would win.

Part of telling your story is understanding the story of the people in your community—you need to weave together a fabric of resistance. This is harder in some ways today because there aren't so many places that serve as public places for conversation about progressive protests. There's been an erosion of public space for discourse. While we've shifted the public sphere in large part online (for good and for ill), it's hard to find novel places for conversation about politics in public spaces (particularly as we've seen the sabotage of Twitter). German beer halls would have libraries in them, so people would read and think and talk. This brought people into the fold. Having a space to talk about politics can also structure conversations between allies. Abolitionists in the United States taught the socialists how to organize, who then taught the first-wave feminists.[5] We're joining a long, eclectic, diverse line of activists, and now we're part of that genealogy. Claim your place on the family tree and start weaving your story with the stories of the past.

Learning from what worked

In these "learning from what worked" sections, we'll flash back to what the activists I spoke with identified as the keys to their success.

For millions of people, the 2016 election created the shock they needed to begin this process. [📢] As the country emerged from its horror, people sought out community. One organizer described an impromptu gathering in her state's capital: "We sat on the Capitol landing's steps. The young woman who was organizing it was a crier, and we did a lot of crying—and it felt really good."[6] An organizer from Texas remarked that the election had ironically, for the first time, shown her she wasn't alone: the progressives in her town sought out one another, determined to be a bulwark against the spread of fascism in the country.

Almost every activist I talked to described being devastated by the results of the 2016 election. Many of them participated in the Women's March, which became a source of strength—a way to reclaim their country and feel like all wasn't lost.[7] This feeling of community followed through to the way that people began to organize once they returned home: "We're offering ways to be a part of a community. This spirit of community involvement . . . a spirit of action." A sense of solidarity and community emerged among people in 2017, which channeled into a heightened rate of organizing: "We don't have the option to ignore this—we're in this together, we can laugh and have wine and support each other and ask weird questions. The group makes me feel empowered; it feels less hopeless," said an activist from the Midwest.

Finding your people is part of the constitutive work of building a movement; even if you're not immediately accomplishing bold cultural and political change, you are still creating the space to make a community, and this matters.

We all enter the struggle at different points—some of us inherit a generational imperative for justice, while others of us come late, turning our sense that "all is not well" into action.[8] Just as our country has different time horizons for movements, so do individual protesters. One organizer's ancestors were the first American activists: her family had hidden gunpowder in barns during the American Revolution. Black and Latinx organizers I spoke with used the language of a multigenerational struggle. They talked about their ancestors, they talked about the future, they focused on the process of liberation. They talked about community building. Part of organizing means telling a story of a movement that continues to evolve.

Tanisha, another Black Lives Matter leader who played a central role in this project, told me: "I was like 'I need to be in Ferguson.'"

Her boss looked at her, told her to go, and that changed the trajectory of her life and protest. She traveled to Canfield Drive, where Michael Brown was shot, and being there "just took me to another level . . . I became a liberation person. We as Black people must be liberated, and obtain freedom and justice over our bodies, our autonomy."

Vietnam was a touchpoint for a many of the activists I talked with. For many retired people, they saw this as part of their narrative of activism that began in the 1960s. However, this time, they wanted it to be different—they didn't want the activism to die, like it had after the war ended. One activist was propelled to activism when her brothers were drafted into the Vietnam War; she became involved with a movement of draft dodgers in Canada. Another woman had stayed active since Vietnam, but then she told me that she was "disgusted with the horizontal hostility of the movement, got disengaged, and then thought 'oh rats I can't remain retired' . . . I strongly suspect that the human race is doomed. But I want to do what I can just in case I'm wrong about that."

Civic engagement and community care are critical parts of any organizing project. One activist had created the first rape crisis center in her town in the 1950s. Another had organized around food justice during college. Sandra, an activist who split her time between Florida and the Northeast, was heavily involved in Clinton's campaign and hoped to secure a position in the Clinton administration. After the 2016 election, she left her job to work full-time as a health care activist, even running for office in her state. She bowed out of the race after a nasty primary, later reflecting that "[e]ven when I was in college in the South, I was marching against the Klan. As a young girl, I was working for the Equal Rights Amendment. That's where I get my good feeling, is being in a rally and talking to people. I don't need to have power. Power has not got me by the throat." [🔊]

One health care activist from the Northwest spoke movingly about how her daughter was the impetus for organizing: "My 16-year-old daughter has autism, and she has a t-shirt that says, 'Feminist AF' and a t-shirt that says the 'Future is Female.' She was starting an internship working with Autistic kids and was wearing her Future is Female shirt. I said, 'Honey, you might want to go change,' and she said, 'Well, I want to make a statement.' And I was like 'Fucking love you, man . . .' She's like a radical feminist. I'm so proud of her."

For others, getting involved in organizing is an existential necessity. Ravi, a Sikh activist, said: "9/11 happened and from a community standpoint or from a perception of me in the world, I went from being an outsider and sometimes laughable or other, into being the enemy and being an eminent threat and being un-American." [📢] After the massacre of Sikhs at the Oak Creek gurdwara in 2012, Ravi's realized that "my government was, I would say not only inept, but willfully disoriented to domestic terrorism and the needs to minority communities in the United States." These stories matter, and are often untold in our country. Listen to them, and use them to understand how oppression is interconnected.

> *Please, people, we have a world to change and we're obviously not doing it.*
>
> —A HEALTH CARE ORGANIZER FROM THE NORTHEAST

But also . . .

As you're finding your path through the world of organizing, we have our to-do lists, but we also have things to avoid. Here are some things to watch out for:

- Instead of saying "you should," say "I will."
- Don't give up on people in the middle.
- Take leadership from people who don't look like you.

Instead of Saying "You Should," Say "I Will"

Even as you're finding your people and your story and your footing, it's important to be surveying the broader cultural landscape. Community work is messy, emotional, complicated work—and there isn't a blueprint for it. Because the job is so sprawling, and things can feel so dark, it's easy to point fingers and tell people what to do (with the best of intentions). Especially for those of you who have been around awhile, it's easy to want to give advice, and talk about what used to work. But that urge to give advice can feel to other people like it's sucking air out of the room, stifling new ideas.

One way to reorient things is to say "I will" instead of "you should." As White people, what will we do? What can I do as a White woman to combat racism in my community? What will I do to stop books from being banned, to stop the blatantly racist crime narrative driven by misinformation? How can I help save the country from racist White people? How can I disrupt the narrative that they tell of our country?

The truth is, when you blur your vision, when you allow multiple voices and multiple stories to come into your view, you learn that lots of people are, right now, getting it right. When you exist hovering between communities, you can see where their world views, their stories, blend, and where there is chafing, and where there are points of friction.

Don't Give up on the Middle

There are people you can't change, but there are people you can—talk to them. About 48 percent of White women identify with the Democratic Party; White women, how can we run up the margins here? How can we convince White women that their fate should lie in being activists, pro-democracy, in being women, not in being White?

Certainly, there is what legendary political scientist Theda Skocpol calls a civil war in White communities that is awkward, uncomfortable, and that we haven't done a very good job of naming or writing about yet. It's clear that those of us from nonminoritized groups need to get our acts together. We need to take ownership for, and call in, the women who are creating disasters across the country in the name of feminism. We need to be clear about what that means. TERFs are not feminists. JK Rowling, that means you.[9] Chimamanda Adichie, that means you too. If people resolutely, in public, use their privilege to violate the principle of inclusivity, they need to leave the ranks. [📢]

Some folks will always vote Republican. But there is a whole swath of folks living in the suburbs, particularly women, who can be persuaded to be activists if they're given a reason, an identity, and a cause—those are the people you should invite and reach out to. Women want access to power so they look for solidarity along race—convince them there's more power to be found if they join the struggle where everyone has more rights. Black activists lead us to a place where our whole community can be well (to paraphrase Brittany Cooper).

Right now, the culture war is purposefully divisive. It attacks trans athletic kids. (Utah tried to pass a law to ban based on one trans student who wanted to participate in sports. TERFs—whether on the right or the left—punch down and have no place in the movement. It's that simple. As Tanisha often told me, what a beautiful place the world would be if we took leadership from trans Black men.) It attacks the books that kids read. It makes people feel selfish for wanting student loan forgiveness. (How does this help plumbers? Asks the party that never helps plumbers.) It writes Black families out of the narrative, withdraws their say over what they want their kids to read, positing that all kids will feel guilty learning about America's past. (What about non-White kids feeling vindicated, feeling seen?) It forces people who to travel to other states for abortion services, effectively banning reproductive care for poor, minoritized, rural folks. It creates silos, which creates false senses of scarcity.

There is a group of people who can be persuaded to help their communities who are sitting on the couch right now: Instead of condemning them for being inactive, we need to get them excited to join the struggle. For folks like these, a sense of civic engagement and of connection to the broader community already existed, but their identity as an activist solidified after the 2016 election. One organizer said, "I really [had] not been involved in politics at all until, of course, Donald Trump got elected." Another activist said she had never been particularly active, but that the everyday effort of resistance made this kind of work meaningful for her in retirement: "Since Trump's election, that's when I just put both feet right in and started just doing everyday work."

If we don't do this—if we don't provide a home and an identity and a sense of purpose and a place where our message is constantly amplified and articulated and welcome people in the middle who are looking for a political home, they're going to become anti-CRT folks. Instead, we grow our tent. We invite them to sit down at the table, even if it wobbles. However, once we call them in, it's our responsibility to educate them. They can't think they are the only game in town. Introduce them to other people doing good work. Educate your neighbors! Show them that the world is big!

Learning from the past

Theda Skocpol, an acclaimed political scientist and analyst of social movements, wrote in 2019 about the fissure among White Americans: "White middle-class resisters abhor the racist and intolerant Trump provocations that appeal to (even thrill) other Americans who are likewise mostly middle-class whites. The Trump wars racking the country right now are in important respects 'a civil war between opposed camps of White Americans—camps whose participants have very divergent understandings of the trajectory and meaning of US history.'" The Women's March helped to highlight that middle-class White America was *not* all conservative, and to bring progressives from their living rooms into the streets.[10]

Clementine, who you'll meet in Step Four, put it this way: "We're just done. We've fucking had it. We had freedom and rights for almost

50 years that we can see are on the chopping block. And women get shit done. We're the ones who have the checklist . . . it's not like there are no men. It's just that we're the ones who are at risk. We're the ones under threat. We're the women who didn't vote for Trump. At least someone in this state has a fucking brain." And yet, in the 2021 runoff between Raphael Warnock and Herschel Walker, only 30 percent of White women voted for the democratic candidate. We have a ways to go. The work isn't hard to identify.

DISPATCHES FROM THE FIELD 6:
MEET ELENA

Elena is a millennial Latinx California native Berkeley grad who now works at a major progressive organization in DC. Here is her story:

> I was born and raised in East Los Angeles and I'm a Mexican, both of my parents are Mexican. My mom's an immigrant, my father was raised in Baja, California, and he's been a farm worker. So, my history, my narrative, my worldview, all that is uniquely embedded in a long history of resistance and migration. The culture that I came up in, you know East LA is so specific. Like our history and our roots as Mexicans in California is really deep. Like we were there before America was, so we have a distinct culture as Chicano. And so, my parents walked out from Garfield High School in the late sixties, early seventies. That was the epicenter of the Chicano Rights Movement [📢] and even though, they didn't grow up telling me about their political activism, it was still deeply embedded in our culture and our ethos and how we engaged with our neighborhood, how we chose not to engage with the cops and how we tried to avoid the sort of like system.

But the experience of learning ethnic studies for the first time and understanding that Columbus was just this mediocre dude that was actually a rapist and like a sociopath and really fucked up and didn't discover shit, like you know just like the frame of reference and how all of the lies that we were told was really an eye-opening experience.

It shouldn't have come as a surprise to anyone that I ended up on this path, but my freshman year I actually started one of the remnants of the Prop 187 youth organizing groups co-teaching an ethnic studies class. Most of these kids who were put into the classroom were considered at risk because they were getting pushed out by the system. And so, like the guidance counselor who had a really good relationship with the teacher who taught that class was helping funnel students through this course, and it was a really great experience.

I mean now that I look back on it, I realize that it was essentially youth organizing and we would not only teach the class, but we were peers. We took an annual field trip to Alcatraz Island and every year we would have a sunrise ceremony with the Indigenous folks. And so, it was like this really beautiful experience I did all through college, and so it really gave me the tools that I needed and the philosophy and the sort of ideology that has carried me throughout my entire career.

But what actually got me into organizing was that I was a waitress working at a local pizzeria. There was something in the air, this was 2006, and so I was noticing, I was like 'all of us, why is this the best job that we could possibly get? Also, what the fuck is going on? Why is this racism, sexism, like why is this all okay just because we're servers, right?'

My manager would come up to me and rub my shoulders and be super-aggressive sexually and there was no recourse. They would cut our hours if we talked back, there was a lot of abuse. I was like, okay so something's going on, right? The American dream doesn't exist, we were told that if we got through college we would have good jobs, we would have health care, we don't have any of this. We have to do something to make these good jobs.

And when I dug a little deeper, I realized there's this organization called the Young Workers United that was specifically organizing immigrants and millennials in the restaurant and retail industry. As a means to sort of reinvigorate the dying labor movement and also because there's some serious shit that needs to be addressed, this was the fastest growing domestic economy and so then jobs needed to be good, and it needed to be addressed.

You know before, this was before Occupy, this was before the analysis around the economy and before the term millennial was coined, so this was one of the first things, this organization was really a pioneer in that. [📢] I ended up doing more and more research. I got really excited about the work that they were doing, joined the organization, applied for a job, got hired, and then six months later became the executive director because I was the stupidest one, I was the only one that would say yes, and then went back and organized the restaurant that I worked at.

And so, we ended up winning better health care coverage and so the workers there before would have to wait two years, now the term limit was like immediate, they had access to it immediately. Their regular raises were more, they specified when people would expect regular raises. It wasn't like the worst restaurant in the area, it was actually a good restaurant, so it didn't take a lot of organizing. They were sort of benevolent masters, but yeah so that was sort of how I got in.

Take Leadership from People Who Don't Look Like You

As we think about existing in a world where people like us are permanently making good trouble, we must think about how we map that world—who are the leaders and who are the supporting cast? Hopefully, you have the chance to be both, depending on circumstance and your expertise. Being a leader is a gift—but it is also a gift to be a collaborator. If we're going to be a big, messy, activist family, we need to learn to take leadership from people from all different backgrounds. The incomparable bell hooks had something to say about this as well: "Many women have said to me, 'We wanted Black women and non-White women to join the movement,' totally unaware of their perception that they somehow 'own' the movement, that they are the 'hosts' inviting us as 'guests.'"

Who's doing the systemic work in your community? What can you learn from them? If *you* are doing systemic work, who are the rapid responders who might be able to help mobilize people and resources, who can be persuaded to use their privilege to support broader calls for freedom? Tanisha reminded me to listen to the lessons that all people have to teach: "When you listen to the most marginalized and uplift the most marginalized, this county would be so beautiful. You listen to those folks, schizophrenic, homeless folks on the streets and you help them, we will be a beautiful country." Community building involves all of us.

Learning from the past

Taking leadership will also help to put what you know in a broader perspective. A common critique I heard from protesters of color was that new activists were so insulated by their privilege, it was difficult for them to accurately understand the stakes of protest in their communities. For example, one member of an immigrant rights group sardonically referred to it as the "Caucasian Shock"; people of color across the country had steeled themselves for the outcome of the 2016 election, but liberals just didn't see it coming because they were so enamored with the idea of Hillary Clinton becoming the next president. Tanisha mused: "I would say that if we all took leadership from Black transwomen we'd be somewhere beautiful. But if you just didn't want to do that, if you took leadership from Black women in general, what a different country this would be."[11]

Even if you're organizing for specific issues, you should know why people are lifelong protesters—know the history of the struggle and resistance. Ask them. Even as you're finding your why, you should remember that people who are also part of this movement are here for different reasons. Some people face an existential threat in our society—we all need to be part of the same liberatory struggle (and not leave til we're all free). As Brittany Cooper says, your feminism is suspect if you're just using it to have access to the same power men have always had.

For folks facing systemic oppression, activism is necessary for survival. As Morgan, who you'll meet in Dispatch 15, told me: "*People in marginalized communities we are literally trying to stay alive all the time.* Almost every trans person I know is a good activist within six months of coming out, just to get through their lives."[12] Rethinking what we ask for from various members of society, and the type of work they are expected to contribute, can help with our project of what Hooker calls "democratic repair."

I often asked activists about membership: How do you find people? Who shows up? And questions of accessibility were almost never raised except by folks who would need accommodations to participate. As one organizer told me, "Organizing work isn't sustainable for a lot of people . . . disability justice gives you a new framework for activism."

Activists with disabilities are often kept out of events because of a lack of accessibility—meeting rooms with stairs that were impossible to navigate, or a lack of accessible bathrooms were barriers to disabled activists becoming part of these groups. One organizer called me outside of our normal interview cycle to talk about her frustration with the lack of attention paid to disability rights in the so-called progressive movement. She had branched off to start her own organization focused on expanding opportunities for people with disabilities to participate fully in society.

Structure matters when it comes to making our efforts accessible. I heard multiple stories about folks who were kept from events because of accessibility issues—from organizations renting buses that weren't handicap accessible to travel to state capitol rallies to having fundraisers and meetings in nonaccessible rooms. (People! How are you having so many meetings in basements and on fourth floors with no elevators?) One activist, a polio survivor, drove 45,000 miles campaigning for a state office with a walker and arm braces, and there were no provisions to even that playing field or lower the barrier to entry for her. Given the lack of accommodations for John Fetterman in the 2022 campaign for the Pennsylvania Senate seat, it's clear we haven't learned how to ensure that political spaces are accessible and welcoming from the organizing town hall to the debate floor.[13]

Again and again, disabled activists had to organize for their lives and to create a space for themselves (mirroring the language of people of color and LGBTQ+ activists as well). One activist described to me, why, though she aligns ideologically with the socialist party, she still votes for Democrats:

> When you're a White male, it's easier to say, 'I'm not going to give my consent or support moderate candidates' because you're not being personally harmed. I'm now being harmed because of the changes to food stamps. I still struggle, I have made a commitment I will not give any monetary support to Democrats . . . but I'm not going to not vote for them.

In Sum:
Take Risks, Get Smarter, Get an Analysis

As you begin to figure out your place in changing the world, you start with finding your why and finding your friends. As you do so, keep the CSI in mind:

Constant—When you discover your "why," and manifest an activist identity, it's not something to turn off. You are learning how to shift into a constant, slow-burning, mode of resistance. By saying "I will" instead of "you should," you're orienting yourself toward action.

Slow—It isn't jumping from one thing to the next, but figuring out where you fit, listening to stories, getting the lay of the land in your town.

Inclusive—Finally, you are using a universal design framework to make sure that everyone can find a seat at your table and you're taking leadership from people who don't look like you (including young and marginalized folk).

Political activism is tricky because it's learning how to lead, how to organize, in public—and that means how to motivate people, how to exercise political and social power, how to stay mobilized yourself. It's a lot, and you're doing it in high-stakes situations, where it's easy to get a lot of things wrong. This means being willing to take risks and being willing to get smarter.

Tanisha, the BLM member, has a favorite question: "What is your analysis?" She asked that question of me, of herself, of other people participating in politics. "I'm like, you wanna take leadership from people who have an analysis on oppression and all the other stuff that impacts people. And in my community they have really been listening."

Activism, no matter what it looks like, pushes you out of your comfort zone. One activist, a hospital nurse, recalled this exchange with a patient during the pandemic. After she asked him to replace his mask because of COVID restrictions he snarked: "Well, I can do that, but I haven't been around Antifa or BLM, so I'm probably good." The nurse retorted, "I've marched with Black Lives Matter three times." I find this story so interesting both because it reveals the utter racist bullshit that you encounter everywhere, even in hospitals. It also shows that women were proud of who they were becoming, and pushing themselves and their community to be more forthright about race.

The murder of George Floyd encouraged many activists to become engaged and educated about the deep reaches of White supremacy. As one activist from the Midwest noted:

> I have participated in anti-racism work for 20 years, but George Floyd's murder inspired me to dive into research this summer. I have always been aware of the need to explore my own privilege, but I have not looked closely at the history of policing. I have witnessed the personal grief of people of color in antiracism training, but I finally realized the crushing burden of dealing with the stress of encounters with the police and the constant tutoring they are expected to do with both allied and adversarial White people.

Although it's easy to dismiss stories like this through a lens of frustration with the newly woke, I argue that it's more productive to make the table wobbly: to hold people to live with their newfound knowledge and convictions. In the case of the activist above, developing empathy and awareness drove her resolve to organize.

Developing an analysis also helps you change your orientation on things; as one civil rights organizer told me, "Trump takes us out of the human rights convention, everybody freaks out. I mean, I also think that's horrible, and it's a terrible mind fuck, but when you stop to think about it, you're like 'what does this actually change?' Because we don't follow it anyway . . . it's like well at least we're not bullshitting anyone anymore. In a fucked-up way, he's the first president not to lie about it." Trump poured gasoline on problems that had been simmering in the American political system for quite a while.

In essence, this chapter has been about claiming your citizenship. We all have the opportunity to share the burden of citizenship. As Juliet Hooker writes: "Democratic sacrifice is supposed to be equally distributed, as is care and concern over the losses suffered by fellow citizens." Activists with privilege, energy, and time need to take it upon themselves to do more of the lifting: How do you more equally distribute these burdens of citizenship but also ensure that the outcomes don't reify those burdens? After you find your why and your people, the next step is to get mobilized: what will you do? How will you do it?

DISPATCHES FROM THE FIELD 7:
LEARNING FROM THE WOMEN'S MARCH

Like Perla, whose life was changed by the Women's March, women across the country took to the streets to protest the 2016 election. Even the act of traveling to the march became deeply significant; activists imparted great significance to the pilgrimage to the Women's March in DC, meeting at airports, on metros, and on 24-hour bus rides with dozens of other women through the deep South. On these trips, pink pussy hats became a highly visible symbol of solidarity. Social media was jammed with pictures of women in airports and on planes—almost all White and wearing pink hats—Southwest Airlines even turned the cabin lights to pink for the occasion. Approximately 4.2 million people appeared on the streets of Washington, DC, and in sister marches all over the country as part of the Women's March. In Washington, the number of people assembled dwarfed the inauguration a few weeks later. Seas of women in pink pussy hats (carrying defiant signs reading "Grab This!") came out to assert that women had not been heard in the election. Recounts of the Women's March have reached a near-mythical status, with participants describing the chanting, the wall-to-wall bodies, the life-sized puppets, and the articulation that, in the words of one participant, "No, this is not the America we know or want it to be."

On an unseasonably warm January day, I joined the Women's March in Lincoln, Nebraska, with my husband, my three-year-old son, and some friends and colleagues. As we marched and the crowd swelled around us, I was taken aback by the visible anger in the usually placid little town. I felt a sense of pride, and also a real feeling of shock that I was not alone in my anger and grief.

The majority of Lincoln voted for Clinton, but surrounding Lancaster County did not; our district stayed red. Nebraska is in the unusual position of splitting its electoral votes: It occasionally gives its Omaha-area vote to Democrats. Obama had carried NE-02 in 2008, but not in 2012. Trump carried the seat in 2016 before Biden won it back in 2020. Nebraska progressives were angry, and they stayed that way. Nationwide, there was a profound sense that rallies were effective and that the Women's March, in particular, had inspired and directed activists. "It was one of the most momentous things I had ever done in my life," one woman commented. Another told me, "Never in my life have I been with that many millions of like-minded, convivial, compassionate people. So, it was very moving. And I would just say . . . I was here. I knew I needed to be there. And not only for me but for my children." There was a sense that "there's hope now" and "we can fix it."

As the protests turned into a sustained resistance after the Women's March, women stayed active: 63 percent of participants at resistance events following the Women's March were women, a much higher level of engagement than in other moments of protests.

MOBILIZE (BUT SLOW YOUR ROLL)

DISPATCHES FROM THE FIELD 8:
MEET DONNA

Donna is a Cherokee activist living in a Plains state. Here is her story.

Okay. Basically, I wouldn't tag myself as being politically active up until recently. Now, with that said, I probably as I think back now, with the roots of my political activism probably came from through the years, I was raised in what could be termed a Sundowner Town. And in essence, there were no people of color in the town, unless they worked there and left at the end of the day. And, so, that was a very odd, you know, but I was not at all personally raised that way, I do have Native American background, I hold a CDIB (Certificate of Indian Blood) card, I'm Cherokee. However, I was not raised knowing I was Cherokee necessarily, that all came about more in adulthood. I believe in separation of church and state and so then as the Trump election came about, I was very . . .

well, I mean many of us, you know, that was a very disturbing night. It just really weighed on me very, very heavy, what we had done as a country and so, the Women's March was starting to develop at that time. I kept feeling I needed to do something and looking at the March and I tried to check out a couple of the groups going [by bus]. I was very back and forth, I had never participated in anything of that magnitude but I very much felt like I had to. And so, I rode that bus to DC. We drove straight through, 24 hours. Got in a few hours of sleep. Got up and got on the bus to take us into the Metro. Went into the March for the day. Came back, caught the Metro, and drove 24 hours back home.

I will tell you that, to this day, it was one of the most momentous things I had ever done in my life. I never heard a cross word. I was shoulder to shoulder jam-packed with people of all ages, all race, all genders. There were many times the crowd needed to move to let police vehicles and others through. Everybody was very amicable. We were all there for the same reason. So, I like to say, that never in my life have I been with that many millions of like-minded, convivial, compassionate people. So, it was very moving. I knew I needed to be there. And not only for me, but for my children. Basically, I am very proud that the Cherokee Nation and I have put these repeatedly out on our pages, they have stepped up the game and have been sending out notices to employees, to all Cherokee Nation citizens, urging everyone to get registered to vote, and vote. The Deputy Chief, personally, last week filmed a video that they put out that they spoke on the Cherokee Nation page, personally asking everyone to do their civic responsibility to get registered to vote. So, they have really been pushing that and that's something that I have not seen in the past.

In the simpler time of the 1980s, before the internet and helicopter parents were really a thing, my twin best friends and I were often left to our own devices. We put that time to good use, watching the *Sound of Music* on repeat. Our copy came on two VHS tapes. On the long road trips that our families would take together (no screens in the minivan) we'd pass the miles by singing the entire score, loudly, from the backseat. We were charming.

Fast forward thirty-some-odd years later, they wanted to watch the movie with my kids. I hesitated, worried about whether it aged well. I'm tired, y'all. I didn't want to have to critique the essence of my childhood. But fear not. There's some obnoxious gender stuff, but on the question of Nazis and authoritarianism, the movie is unequivocal—and somehow feels bold. In one scene, Maria and Captain Von Trapp return from their honeymoon to find the Nazi flag hanging from their roof. As the captain unceremoniously rips up the flag, Max (their morally squishy manager) murmurs to Maria, "He's got to pretend to work with these people. You must convince him." To which Maria replies, "I can't ask him to be less than he is." Yes, Maria! Preach, Julie![1] This feels particularly daring to me from the vantage of a media climate that insists on squinting sideways to see, and cover, Trump as a "normal" politician.

How can we be as brave as the moment demands? Mr. Rogers tells us to look for the helpers, and I think that's probably right. We can also look for bravery (and its absence).[2] Alexei Navalny, for example, is incredibly brave. He was the face of the Russian opposition. He went *back* to Russia to lead the opposition after he was poisoned. (The poison, friends, was put in his undies.) When the Russian regime murdered Navalny in a prison inside the Arctic Circle in 2024, he had one final message for his supporters: "You're not allowed to give up."[3] Days later, Yulia Navalnaya, spoke at the Munich Security Conference, challenging the global community to defeat Putin. That, friends, is bravery.[4]

My friend, a prolific Indonesian peace activist and scholar, is fond of reminding me that Gene Sharp (1973) offers 193 methods of nonviolent resistance. She's engaged in most of them at one point or another—dance-ins, die-ins, sit-ins, letter writing, large-scale protest as she's agitated for a more democratic Indonesia. She worries that when people hear "protest," they think marches, and that limits the repertoire of possibilities. Instead, she lives her life with this abiding commitment to peace. She loves board games, but won't ever be the aggressor (even when playing Risk). She finds smarter, strategic ways to win. I've learned a lot from her, and not least from her unwavering belief in nonviolence.[5] Nerds, book club lovers, people with too many degrees—this is our time to reimagine the world of community building. Everything we do can be protest if we think of it through an oppositional lens. This chapter gives you some concrete ideas about how to mobilize: what action *looks like*.[6] Showing up for democracy in any form counts—but as a people we need to stay engaged.

Do this . . .

Let's get to work! Here's our to-do list.

- Get mad.
- Appeal to people's strengths.
- Develop inclusive models of protest.
- Write a blueprint for action.
- Don't underestimate the power of discomfort.
- How will this become your life?

Get Mad

We meet every Monday night . . . It's like going to Alcoholics Anonymous. You just feel so good when you're done.

—AN INDIVISIBLE LEADER FROM THE SOUTHWEST, 2018

Civility is nonsense. One thing that the far right does well is to channel a sense of anger—we need to be mad too, stay mad, and use it to guide a framework for action.

Shock can create resolve and a need to act. Rebecca Traister's remarkable book *Good and Mad* concludes: "Don't *ever* let them talk you out of being mad again." After all women, particularly Black women, are often punished for their anger, shunned or made into harpies for their anger, accused of being emotional and irrational for their anger.

Consider this line from Traister's book:

> Even when things were bad, a non-confrontational approach was preferable, for strategic, aesthetic, and moral reasons. So I was funny! And playful, cheeky, ironic, knowing! I worked to make it clear that I am a fun person who enjoys friends and beer and laughter. I took great care to be nice and respectful to opposing viewpoints . . . . Many of us who may have covered our fury in humor have occasionally found ourselves exploding.

So we . . . soften. Dodge. Compromise. Are collegial. Make jokes.[7] And let those who hold power win the battle for the cultural tenor.

And it's not just women. For years I had my classes read Ta-Nehisi Coates's gorgeous *Between the World and Me*. It shocked them, worried them. They often would retreat into the comfort zone of the "angry Black man" trope. "Why is Coates so mad?" they would ask. "Why is he mad at all White people?"

Do we need to be angry all of the time? Of course not. But when we are angry, we can use it pragmatically, for justice. One of the major insights of the excellent book Deva Woodly's *Reckoning*, which provides a political analysis of Black Lives Matter, is that there could be a pragmatic dimension to social movements. Although movements can be radical and idealistic, if protests are going to succeed, they must be ruthlessly pragmatic. It's worth considering different theories of power and how it flows between the state and protesters: we're not waiting for people to change their minds and be persuaded by protests—*it's not an invitation to those who are stripping rights away to join us.* However, we don't want to be confined by our anger. We want it to be a strategy, not a limiting device.[8]

Disrupt the sense of business as usual. Pierce the veneer of civility. If you're trying to make change by hoping that you can persuade your jailors to turn over the keys (or burn the prison down), you're always going to decide *not* to be angry (and it won't work—too much of their self-identity and worldview is embedded in those cells staying shut). If you want to dismantle the prison-industrial complex, and you believe abolition is the only path to freedom, you need to be angry—and use that to persuade other people that anger (and love) is their path to freedom. Whatever your issue is, channel your anger, spite, rage toward building a better world.

Learning from what worked

The Women's March inspired years of activism from one single day of protest *because* it gave an outlet for anger, and then encouraged people to stay mad. Perhaps if Trump had orchestrated a more boring, conventional, bipartisan beginning to his presidency, things might have been different, but because people were angry, they stayed engaged. They became organized.

Once activists returned home, the Women's March created a sense of comradery amongst angry folks who channeled that rage into action. For many women, gender was the motivating impulse behind their activism: the women became activists because they knew that their rights, particularly abortion rights, were under attack. Sandra, an activist from the Northeast, observed that: "#MeToo had a lot to do with the post-election resistance, but this has been a movement building for 30 years. In living memory women only had their husband's credit. This sense of 'no, we're not going to put up with that!' was very galvanizing—a unifying force for women." [📢] The Women's March rolled into the protests against the travel ban . . . and people kept turning out.

Appeal to People's Strengths

Grab a pen, right now, and write down 10 things you're good at. Don't roll your eyes and half make a list in your head. Actually write it down.

Here are mine:

- I'm a good writer.
- I'm good at organizing people.
- I'm a pretty good public speaker.
- I'm good at organizing ideas.
- I'm a very good editor.
- I'm okay at computer stuff/websites—not an expert but better than a lot of people.

- I'm really good at seeing what other people are good at and including everyone in conversations.
- I'm an effective manager.
- I'm good at synthesizing information.
- I'm quite good at research.
- I'm a good debater/good at thinking of strategies.
- I'm a good teacher.
- Okay, so that was a little awkward, but I even got 11!

Now, circle three or four of these and break them into subskills: I'm a good writer—which means I'm good at writing position papers, letters to the editor, SEO heads, blog posts, books, speeches . . . you get the idea. This can give you a sense of ways you can help build your community.

Now, write down five things you really hate doing. Mine are:

- Talking on the phone
- Asking strangers for things
- Dealing with money
- Keeping my cool when strangers say or text mean things
- Having long conversations where nothing is resolved

Many of these are rooted in anxiety, which I get—and it's real for me. And if you're going to ask me to do these, maybe I will once or twice—I've knocked on my share of doors and worked call centers and done text banking, but I really hate it and it won't be sustainable. This is important to keep in mind. Maybe there's *one* weekend you need everyone knocking on doors, even your introverts: make the ask carefully. As I'm writing, my shoulders are tensing . . . I'm feeling resistance to the very idea of canvassing. I can do it in an emergency, but it's not long-term sustainable for me.

In the lead-up to the 2016 election, we spent time in Iowa, knocking on doors and hoping against hope that the state might, in fact, be swingier than it seemed. We knocked on the door of one house, and a woman yelled at us "I'm not telling you how I'm voting!" We moved on, pushing our stroller through suburban streets, hoping to find at least a few friendly Clinton voters. As we were getting ready to leave, the same woman drove up to us. "Can you turn in my ballot for me?" "Sure," we replied. She leaned out the window, dropped it on the stroller, and drove off. That ballot, a sword of Damocles, taunted us. We wondered if she'd decided to vote for Clinton or just liked the idea of us turning in a Trump ballot. But I digress.

Now—the wonderful thing about humanity is that some of you very much love these things! If someone texts you "erase my number, you progressive scum,"[9] it's like water off a duck's back! Some of you love hosting fundraisers and raising money from the well-financed among us. I'm so super glad you exist in this world . . . because it's just not me.

As you start figuring out how to sustain a group, doing these skill exercises are important. What are people's skills? Where are they connected, both in the community and online? How can you use those things? (I've heard activists relate this to Myers-Briggs or to Enneagram scores—probably both pseudoscience, but maybe useful heuristics!)

If you're going to have long meetings and then ask a bunch of introverts to knock on doors, you're going to lose your people. If you're going to have long meetings, ask your introverts to do research, do some writing of scripts, and then maybe participate in one day of door knocking at the very end, they'll be far more likely to stick around. And if you're going to tell a bunch of extroverted organizers that we need to study the issue, then those folks need to have an outlet they're working toward where they can externally process what they're learning. Figure out who your people are, and put them to work!

Learning from what worked

Most of the Indivisible groups I spoke to had leadership teams and subcommittees based on their tasks or their issues (such as a state issues group, a federal issues group, a direct-action team, and virtual campaigning). Because these groups were new, they were thoughtful about ways members could help them achieve their goals. For example, many leaders helped their members use their analytical skills to motivate volunteers. As one community builder put it, "I'm not the type of person who does door knocking; I'm good at behind-the-scenes stuff." They played to the strengths of different members—in their ranks, they identified people who excelled at reading bills, connecting groups, or strategic planning.

Professions are a deep pool of talents: schoolteachers can talk and educate, writers can write letters to the editor, folks in finance can fundraise. By mapping talents, the groups could then make decisions about where to put their energy. One group with skilled data analysts created a progressive version of the Partisan Voter Index published by the Cook Political Report. They scored the districts in their state in terms of likelihood to flip, evaluated downstream races, and made recommendations for where to focus canvassing efforts. A reason to get the data nerds to come work with you!

Develop Inclusive Models of Protest

Stop for a second and listen to the song that ends Act I of *Hamilton*— "Non-Stop." This song was an earworm as I wrote this book because I constantly feel like I'm running out of time: to get this book published, to save democracy (and I've been accused of *thinking* I'm the smartest person in the room as well). But look: we need to commit to a generational struggle.

Everything you do can help build your community—we need to let a million flowers bloom. Some people will show up to big protests once—great. We need those people, we need their energy, we need their bodies in the street. Some people will do that and then go hyperlocal, being involved with changing their school system, being involved

with local environmental initiatives. If they're doing it with an oppositional consciousness, each form of microresistance counts.

We need to develop inclusive models of what it looks like to organize for change in our communities. At its core, anything we do to
improve parts of the little slices of our world (without impinging on the
rights of others) is the kind of work we need to do. A little league coach
having a league-wide conversation about anti-bullying and building
the self-esteems of child athletes is creating conditions for a more just
corner or their world. A sexual assault survivor who talks with other
people from her church school about their experiences and petitions
the media to pay attention is also creating change. People who hold
protests against a homeless shelter being built in their community are
not—they are engaging in protectionist behavior without creating conditions for a more just world.[10]

You might feel like you need to be everywhere—but only one issue
is fine. Many books that are like this follow this story of one group: an
environmentalist group, or a women's rights group, or an anti-human
trafficking group. I love those books because you get to meet folks
who are giant issue-oriented nerds. Shannon Watts, one of my heroes,
is a nerd for ending gun violence. It's her thing. Ady Barkan, another
one of my heroes, had dedicated his like to health care. You might have
friends who focus on abortion or environmentalism or education—
those are all amazing issues. You also might be a one-issue person. Your
issue might be sweatshops. Housing. Memory and Confederate monuments. Educational access and equity. *We need you.* We need the people
who are the buoys for every issue, who are willing to be the central
node in activist networks and keep track of where politicians are and
who's willing to donate money. We need single-issue activists who have
dedicated their lives to making that small thing better.[11]

Learning from what worked

Sometimes, creating these conditions for change can be loud and highly visible. The most visible form of activism is obviously taking to the streets, either through mass marches (Women's March) or prolonged periods of civil disobedience. One activist told me: "We need people in the streets. A Bastille Day." Others imagined what would happen if conflict between the far right and the resistance escalated, like we saw in Portland—or if there were draconian measures taken against protesters.[12] As one organizer told me: "We are ticking now into civil disobedience. You should put your body where your brain is. Put your body out there. I'm not afraid to put myself into scary situations so I feel like I'm contributing in some way." Of course, this is what we saw (at least for a while) during the protests after George Floyd's death.

Other times, community building looks different, and can be more like education.[13] One group took a pilgrimage from the Northwest to the South, doing a deep dive into the racial history. As one organizer told me: "You build a bond that is strong, and then it builds more around what's happening politically—it brought us collectively to a different place than where other groups are." Her group met Anthony Ray Hinton, the man wrongly convicted of murder in 1985 who now does anti-racism work, went to a lynching site, and explored the legacy of racism in the United States. After encountering the work he is doing to address the racism in the justice system, particularly in terms of who gets sent to death row, they took that back into their communities. She told me: "It's a lot of retired White people that live in the suburbs, but that want to do something. They don't want to just complain about what's happening, they want to actually do something." Although there are dangers in creating spots of disaster tourism, and certainly there are problems in their own communities that need tending to, there's something to be said about giving people the opportunities to explore the parts of the country they simply have no idea about. Cultivate empathy.

Write a Blueprint for Action

I don't just want to sit on my ass and talk with other like-minded people. I want to see action.

—AN INDIVISIBLE ACTIVIST FROM
THE NORTHEAST, 2018

Like a lot of principles related to slow organizing, there is value in the routine, in the ritual and repetition (I learned recently that ritual and art have the same early root, and I love this because this book could also be called *The Art of Changing the World*). You need to commit to change. In your crowded life, anything optional falls off the calendar—it just will. If you say, "I'll go when I can," you'll never go. You'll schedule doctor's appointments or sign the kids up for that night of soccer or just decide to grab dinner with the friend that you can never quite sync your calendar with. You won't do it. And I get it. In order to create a sense of forward momentum, you need to create accountability mechanisms or a space that protects your organizing: How will you keep yourself engaged? How will you make sure that you don't let that time or commitment become optional? One way is to make sure there are action steps, and that these action steps—complete with celebrating incremental wins—are programmed into the DNA of your organization. The other way is to make it somewhere you *want* to be.

One of the great mysteries of organizing is how movements spread. One day there are five people protesting . . . then a hundred . . . then thousands. How does that needle tip? I have to admit that, when I first heard of the Women's March, I got it wrong. I assumed that people would go back to business as normal—not that there would be a spillover or cascade effect that got everyone into the streets protesting.[14] But this organizing clearly worked. For instance, one activist told me: "There are more progressive people out there than I ever really anticipated—I think they had just been silent because it had been such a red state." These activists looked to each other to see that progressive activism in red states wasn't dead, but also to see if it was worth their energy to try to change things.[15]

Learning from what worked

Groups that weren't focused on action and change fizzled quickly. One former member of an Indivisible group who later pivoted to local organizing stopped going to meetings: "It was a bunch of people getting together and venting. We did a presentation on what to do if people encounter racism, but beyond that, my fiancé and I felt it was pretty ineffectual." Georgie, who you met in Dispatches from the Field 4, shared her experience with organizations that weren't focused on action: "I got involved with a pro-choice group which was basically kind of like having meetings to talk about what they were going to do at the next meeting, which I found really annoying."

Activists from across the country channeled their energy and talents into restoring their communities and making them whole as part of the strategy for reclaiming their country. One resistance group based their activism on the ACT UP organizing strategy from the 1980s: "Let's have one act, go in there with one ask, and have it be low-hanging fruit, and actually do it." Looking at highly specific examples of successful protest in the past provided a model for resisting in the strange new world.

DISPATCHES FROM THE FIELD 9:
WE'RE INDIVISIBLE

After the Women's March, different organizing groups popped up across the country, including Indivisible chapters, inspired by a handbook written by former congressional staffers, Leah Greenberg, Ezra Levin, and Angel Padilla, who published a Google Doc in December 2016 entitled "Indivisible: A Practical Guide for Resisting the Trump Agenda," based on the Tea Party model of mobilization (Levin et al., 2016). This guide went viral, and the organization institutionalized—they developed a DC chapter, established a 501(c)(4), and began to cultivate grassroots chapters.

Chapters popped up across the country. They began meeting in community centers and basements, in coffee shops and gymnasiums. Six thousand local Indivisible chapters were registered on the website by 2018. The number of branches exceeded those of Tea Party groups from the Obama years, with just as wide a geographical distribution.

The newly formed Indivisible groups got to work, organizing weekly protests at the offices of their members of Congress, familiarizing themselves with state legislative procedure and bill dockets, and mobilizing themselves as a force to resist the Republican agenda. And though causality is difficult to assess, the Resistance racked up quite a list of wins, virtually shutting down Congress from 2016 to 2018 (which is particularly impressive when you consider that the Republicans had a unified government, and pretty much all they could agree on was a tax bill).

At least at first, many groups did not consult organizations comprised of Black and other marginalized people and other far-left organizations already in place in many cities and towns. Although the emergence of Indivisible and other similar groups breathed new life into the protest space in some places, providing an avenue for allyship and resource allocation, considerable conflict also emerged within the progressive landscape as experienced organizers tried to preserve the work they had already done.

As Americans across the country struggled to foment and sustain resistance, they realized that their civics education had ill-prepared them for the work. In a post-modern activist landscape without clear leaders, it was hard for many to know where to begin. As one activist put it, "We needed a model of direct action and a blueprint to resist." Indivisible attracted people because it was a source of education— it taught people how to write letters, what resistance looked like, and focused on grassroots mobilization—it was like a plug-and-play social movement in a box. One organizer said, "I didn't have any experience, and it just took work willing to figure out what to do about Trump. Co-founding Indivisible is often where a lot of Indivisible folks came from, not really knowing the organizing landscape at all. And so, the Indivisible guide appeals to us because it's so pragmatic when everyone was wondering what to do. And it just sort of had, ya know, easy answers. I mean, not easy, but very concrete steps." The guide allowed the proliferation of small, local groups to immediately organize around the United States.

Indivisible also succeeded because it was highly flexible: state-level chapters, LGBT chapters, women's chapters, and district chapters all formed. Some groups dissolved, some merged, and some became Facebook shells to share memes but did little organizing. Others became robust organizations that raised serious money and mobilizing thousands of activists to make calls or show up at protests.

Indivisible appealed to new activists, particularly the Women's March participants, because of its focus on direct action; as one organizer told me: "If I'm giving up my livelihood [for activism] I don't just want to sit on my ass and talk with other like-minded people. I want to see action . . . I was very drawn to confronting these Republicans and moderate Dems, and other people, these do-nothing people, when they would go home for their breaks. The people in Congress, confronting them in town halls."

DISPATCHES FROM THE FIELD 10:
ACA AND THE FIGHT FOR THE NATION'S HEALTH

Many of the organizers I interviewed had long histories as health care organizers. One health care activist who worked for Clinton told me that people kept trying to use whether she worked for Clinton or Bernie as a litmus test. Her Clinton friends were surprised she joined Our Revolution, and Bernie's supporters tried to use her service on Clinton's campaign to disqualify her as an activist. [📢] She says, "I will go any place at any time to talk about universal health care. And I'm okay because I'm issue-oriented, that I get a pass."

Nothing did more to secure the resistance—Indivisible and beyond—as the major organizing force than the showdown over the ACA. [📢] As I interviewed activists and watched the battle over health care unfold, the issue became intensely personal to me. Many of these activists had cut their teeth on health care. One woman I interviewed in New England had founded a free clinic in the seventies, related to a commune in New England. An elderly gentleman from California recounted being arrested twice, once for shutting down a clinic and once at a Congress member's office, both over Medicare for All. Another told me her first job out of college was organizing for health care reform. As one activist put it: "The thing that probably propelled me more than any other issue was this administration's intended destruction of the Affordable Care Act, and all the other rights and gains that we've made. Being somebody that was actually in Washington and working on that, seeing this administration and this Congress try to take that a part infuriated me . . . I worked on helping with people that were arrested at that time . . . my husband went down, and was arrested with a group of clergy . . . people were being pulled out of the capitol and arrested, disabled people. It was horrific to watch."

And health care—in both likely and unlikely ways—was the story of the 2018 election. Although countless people have written about it, I think it's worth considering the ways in which health care became a common theme, and a winning issue, for activists in 2017 and 2018, and then formed the backbone of the Democratic message going into 2020. ACA was also proof that the resistance model could work—that it could exert enough pressure to affect politics.

Most of the GOP ran on repealing the Affordable Care Act. After the bill to repeal Obamacare passed the House I really thought it was going to happen in the Senate (I sat on the edge of my bed, chewing my nails, when John McCain cast the final vote to save health care in our country).

The Democratic Socialists of America (DSA) participated in canvassing for a Medicare for All campaign: "That's a great platform for doing in-depth canvassing. It gives you a reason to go to people's doors, to talk to them about health care, which is something everybody is concerned about. And I think that's how we have to . . . a better way of approaching people rather than just dismissing this conspiracy stuff is that you have a legitimate reason for talking to people about something that people are really concerned about."

As one activist told me, the deep canvassing leads to the kind of relationships that can create culture shifts: "I think that's really the only way we can then defeat some of that conspiracy stuff, is you have to develop that trust relationship where you have an honest interaction with people . . . and I think through community organizing, in the old sense of the word, it's a long game. And it requires people staying invested, and realizing that this is not something you just turn around instantaneously."

One group was able to recruit around ten new members a week because of their dedication to *doing* something, instead of just talking about stuff; as a member told me: "We turn that energy and disgust into actions and activities, we raise money, and we go do it."

As we look at what worked for previous generations of protesters, we should think critically about how to expend our energy. Even if the party strategically aligns itself with "moderates" in order to get certain things accomplished (cough, Joe Manchin), we still need to be clear that all politicians need to pressure in order to vote for an agenda that puts people and the environment first. In blue states, protesters tried to mobilize their members of Congress to be aggressive defenders of progressive values; as one Indivisible leader told me: "We might have B+ senators, but we want to push them—our job as constituents is to push them to be better . . . and remind folks that this is not usual." Group leaders also described how their organization learned over time, figuring out which strategies worked in red versus blue areas.

One California activist shared that her group showed up at Adam Schiff's (CA-28) office shortly after the election and received a hostile reception: The staffers were unprepared for the new normal of pressure from the Resistance. Schiff thought of himself as one of the good guys—why were protesters targeting *him?* Indivisible had shown up ready to apply the same pressure techniques as one would to a Republican member of Congress, but quickly realized they needed to cool that down. Both members of Congress and protesters were learning to live in this new world of resistance. Someone from a blue state remarked: "We have two pretty quiet senators who are quite powerful, but the way they've been doing business on the down-low behind the scenes, whereas what this moment demands is being a leader. We're trying to movement build." Activists saw a real path forward for connecting organizing with politics. They pointed to Pramila Jayapal, a political-organizer-turned-Congress member from Seattle, as inspiration: "She's an organizer, coalition builder, on the ground, she's visible." Jayapal's participation in demonstrations against the travel ban was particularly salient to her constituents, giving her credibility as an organizer first and a politician second.[16]

There was a sense that the progressives didn't know quite what to do with their energy—they wanted to influence elections, but other than running up the margins, that was hard to do. Some built coalitions in red parts of their state, traveling to adopt different local or statewide races and raise money and canvas there. Others adopted races across state lines through organizations like Sister District.

One Californian group chose to target their then-first term democratic Senator Kamala Harris; given her history as a prosecutor, the group felt the need to put heavy pressure on her from the beginning: "We were on a first-name basis with every single person in [her] office, and we actually got to meet her with she did a town hall," one organizer told me. However, after her first year in the Senate, they decided to turn their attention elsewhere: "Kamala Harris is great; she's never gonna be as progressive as I want her to be, but she's pretty damn good, and I don't need to keep my feet on her as much, I can pivot." Similarly, an Indivisible chapter from the Bay Area reached out to Hawaii Indivisibles and began sharing information about judicial nominees. Hawaii Indivisible began putting pressure on democratic Senator Mazie Hirono to take firmer stances against judicial nominees, which she did.

To avoid duplication of efforts, neighboring Indivisible groups found ways to work together strategically or to specialize: in California, Indivisible East Bay conducted judicial research and shared this information as an action statement whenever there was an important court case or a problematic nominee. In Minnesota and Texas, statewide Indivisible chapters were formed to monitor the state legislature and send this information to local chapters, freeing local chapters to engage in varied forms of activism. And, as one organizer reminded me, all good politics is local: "Your local politics could actually change your community and how it looks. We need make sure that even if somebody who is Satan wins, your local politics still protects you."

A member of the Minnesota Indivisible group said, "We realized that what we needed to do is change the Republican-controlled legislature because it didn't align with our values." They shifted their focus, in part, to vetting and supporting progressive candidates for the legislature; they succeeded in flipping the Minnesota House from red to blue.

Here are some stories that stuck with me of what the energy for change can accomplish:

- One person was so furious about developments in his area that he started visiting city council offices until they agreed to work with him on a plan to protect bird sanctuaries from new development.
- Another activist represented a bus rider's union trying to strengthen public transit in their town.
- A member of Black Lives Matter started a breakfast and books program that became a type of community therapy: community building with a focus on wellness. The creator of these events told me: "White people say how can we help—it's called creative reparations. Give me books. Bring the cereal—I need you think and then you'll be able to give to this movement."
- Disability activists poured their energy into making the world accessible for folks. They worked on projects such as advocating for accessible restrooms and meeting areas in public places and petitioning the housing condo association to add equitable housing.
- A Black Lives Matter group threatened to close the Tappan Zee Bridge because New York's Governor Cuomo refused to meet with them to discuss the death of Black trans women in New York. Tanisha told me about her organizing of Black trans women: "I hear their horrors . . ." she told me. "How do we navigate [our community] as Black women, like not being heard, not being seen, raped, beat up." Even though they didn't take the bridge, they earned media coverage and continued the conversation about the plight of Black women in the state.

DISPATCHES FROM THE FIELD 11:
MEET ROGER

Roger, a lawyer from the Midwest, decided to engage full time in protest after the 2016 election. Here is his story:

> After Trump was elected I decided that I wanted to do something to try and change that, so I decided I would quit my job and do community organizing full time. My wife is a school principal and we have a lot of empathy for those vulnerable members of the population who don't have the social capital and the political power to protect themselves I tried to get involved while I was working but my job was just too demanding, so I couldn't really get substantively involved, so I think it was the travel, the travel ban or the Muslim ban that was sort of the last straw. So, we just sat down and sort of talked career options then. Sort of realizing that this seemed like a big moment in time where people who are privileged and had power committed to step up, so we decided that that's what we do. [📢]
>
> The first day, I explored a little bit what was happening to try and say where I could fit in and contribute constructively. I started attending protests and marches, and tried to see if there were ways that I could use my legal expertise.
>
> Eventually I joined a local Indivisible group, and one of the leaders of that group expressed frustration that they were focused on national issues and people kept asking about state-level issues, so I said well let's start a group focused on state-level issues, and that's basically what we did.

Don't Underestimate the Power of Discomfort

In 2018, during the second long, tragic summer of locking babies in cages away from their parents, I went to a Close the Camp protest in Austin. The speaker began: "Thank you for looking. They are counting on us looking away." I was standing in line for the bathroom, thinking about that, and a woman struck up a conversation: "Until today, I'd never thought of those places as concentration camps—that's what they are. We have work to do."

How does change happen—how do people change their minds about big things like social justice issues? For a long time, the theory was that people changed their minds because moral arguments and a healthy sense of shame persuaded them. This story feels good, because there's redemption in it—you can persuade people to come to your side. And this is sometimes undoubtedly the case. For example, there's at least some evidence that having a gay child pushes Republicans to the left on issues of marriage equality (although this is problematic both because you should be able to understand why people want rights even if they aren't members of your family, *and* because everyone knows someone who is gay and the Republican Party is still in the dark ages. But I digress).

However, there is scant evidence that shame and persuasion *actually* work to change the world, at least by themselves. Instead, we need to lean on a different theory of change: discomfort. We need to make people squirm if we're going to convince them to change (and this means squirming ourselves). We can't keep our activism confined to polite politics. People are persuaded because their privilege is interrupted. We need to be more like France,[17] and ignore the people who tell us only to protest politely. Civility doesn't meet us halfway. Civility leads to Brett Kavanaugh on the court. [📢] We need to create discomfort.[18]

The implications are pretty clear: the powerful rely on the consent of the governed to get away with things. We're all complicit by ignoring facts that make us uncomfortable—like when we watch the 2022

World Cup in Qatar knowing that some 15,000 migrants were killed to make those soccer stadiums—this is what Hayward means by motivated ignorance.[19]

The bar to creating that discomfort is lower than you think. Supreme Court justices can ignore a million people in the streets, but they *hate* having dinner interrupted.[20] The 2023 Supreme Court term, like 2022, was terrifying from a rights perspective, but instructive in terms of the extent to which the justices care—a lot—about public opinion.[21]

Because the bar for creating discomfort is so low, so is the threshold for public pressure actually making a difference. I was talking to an education lobbyist from a small state, who recounted a social media campaign she was leading against charter schools. She ran into a state representative from her district, who said, "Okay, okay, we get it. We're getting slammed with calls. We're voting against it—have them stop calling us." And the lobbyist felt really proud of herself—after all, she'd won, by mobilizing opposition to a bill that was going to be bad for education in the state! "Just out of curiosity, how many calls did you get?" the lobbyist asked. "The phone has been ringing off the hook—we must have gotten like 25 calls!" replied the staffer. The squeaky wheel, causing discomfort, made change.

That story stuck with me because of how low the bar is for actually making change. Over four years, civil society in the United States battled the Trump administration to a draw, at least legislatively. Other than their awful tax bill, they didn't get much done. A low level of sustained pressure on local levels can have outsized effects on state and national politics.[22] Friends, you had your congressmembers on speed dial a few years ago—time to update those contacts and start calling again.

So: Be loud. Take up space. Make your demands. Withdraw your consent.[23]

How Will This Become Your Life?

In his astonishing essay "The Power of the Powerless," Václav Havel, one of the leaders of the anti-communist movement in Czechoslovakia, talks about the power of the greengrocer to bring down a communist regime. [📢] The story goes like this. Every month, the communist party sends all the grocers a sign to hang in their windows as a visual display of solidarity with the regime. One month, the greengrocer decides not to hang a "Workers of the World, Unite!" sign in his window. That small act of resistance is enough to sow seeds of doubt that crumble the entire regime.[24]

Like the greengrocer, we all need to commit to living a life of (at least low-key) dissidents or revolutionaries. This looks different for different people. For some people, this is writing, bearing witness, documenting. For others, it means becoming a professional organizer. Still others affiliate with civil society by volunteering for Planned Parenthood or food banks in town. By conscientiously modulating how much energy we spend, we can hopefully avoid getting burned out.

If you're not motivated by the quiet anti-communist resistance of shopkeeps, let Taylor Swift inspire you. When Big Machine Records wouldn't let her out of what everyone knew was a raw deal (they owned the master records of her first 13 albums, a deal she signed at 15 years old), she set out to rerecord *every.single.one* of her songs from scratch so that she owned the copyright (please pause and listen to "Mean" [Taylor's Version] and then come back with a new appreciation of the power of spite). She even turned down a Super Bowl halftime performance so she could finish recording her back catalog. Please, let that energy drive you to make this world a better place.

Micro forms of resistance—the *slow* part of the slow organizing—will hopefully keep you from getting burned out. When you study the big moments of change—the Arab Springs and the March on Washington, and you often wonder how those happened. [📢] They happened because of a million small acts helped create a fabric of resistance that made people want to turn out.

We need to adjust our time horizon and what counts as a win. When my husband helps immigrants study for and then pass citizenship tests, his metric can't be whether he has transformed the refugee system. He does it because he believes in a country made stronger by immigrants, and as a way to welcome new families. When you go build a house, you don't measure that by whether you've solved the housing problem. Now, I know what you're saying—we need to focus on systemic change. Not just putting a Band-Aid on a bullet wound and feeling great about ourselves for showing up one Thursday every November to give some turkey to folks. This is why I'm not talking service—I'm talking resistance.

Resistance can become part of your everyday life. When Emilia was in preschool, we got the class calendar for the next month, and it included a visit from a police officer. I wrote an email opting her out (we're not participating in copaganda when the preschool-to-prison pipeline looks the way it does in NYC). And her teacher called to find out why, and I said I wasn't comfortable with police doing public relations events in preschool, and then arresting kids in high school. Police don't belong in schools, and I don't want my kid encountering the warm and cozy police officer now and being oblivious to the way they abuse their power later.[25] Her teacher (who was amazing) totally understood. "Oh, I remember reading about that school-to-prison pipeline in school!" she said.

I try very hard not to be a helicopter parent, but instead to limit my ire to systemic injustices I'd like to see changed. We also opt out of homework—not all of it, not always, but in kindergarten we wouldn't do more than 10 minutes plus reading. We let our kids choose whether to wear the school uniform (it's a public school). For our kids to be whole people, they need time to bake and run and yes, make their own fashion mistakes and watch television. Opting out is a powerful force—we're not asking someone to change, we're just abstaining, but in a way that we create a little bit of friction where there was none.

What we're doing is nudging. I'm not very good at all of this. I'm much better at kicking my husband and kids out and cleaning the house from top to bottom over a weekend than doing the small five-minute routines that would make it unnecessary to kick them out. But we need those micro-routines to keep our energy up. Through small acts of resistance, small nudges, small ways you're keeping things a little bit less civilized. Become un—or at least less—governable.[26]

Learning from what worked

We know that Republicans think incrementally. They think in terms of 50-year plans, and know that micro-actions are bringing them closer to the promised land of coopting state legislatures. Protesters also reminded me of the importance of doing underground work: "We have to do a little more underground work. We have to do what we can to find wrinkles in the power to be able to get our own local power back."

One day, on a visit to Houston, my sister-in-law mentioned her mother would be late to lunch because a "Stop Trump" protest had popped up, and she needed to drop by first. Resistance had become part of people's everyday calendars, to be fit in between grocery store trips and lunch dates.[27]

As we're getting things done, participating in slow organizing, learning to take up space and from what worked before, we can also be sure not to make the same mistakes that plagued the people who came before us.

Early on, activists tested the water with surprising wins that encouraged them to push further. One activist recounted early success on behalf of his Indivisible chapter to oppose a bill on redistricting: "Legislators that we know were perplexed about why this bill got so much attention." But it worked—this local Indivisible had taken an obscure bill and put their energy behind defeating it—and showed they could win.

Although groups were reluctant to claim total credit for the defeat of bills like this, they were still buoyed by the victory. This enthusiasm compelled action in other areas as well, including the strategy of "adopting" electoral races in other areas and channeling resources toward them. One California-based resistance group wrote 95 postcards for the 2017 Oklahoma special election in support of Allison Ikley-Freeman, an openly lesbian candidate from west Tulsa. As one California organizer remarked: "I've found a renewed appreciation of democracy . . . there have been some races that I've worked in recently that were won by a couple of hundred votes. A vote does make a difference, and by being active, you can make a difference." Ikley-Freeman won by *29 votes* (2234 to 2205 ballots). The California organizer mused: "With margins that small, those 95 postcards could have really made a difference."

But also . . .

Even as we're getting things done, we also have a list of ". . . but alsos":

- Don't miss the forest for the trees.
- Don't mobilize over people.
- The power of yes, and . . .

Don't Miss the Forest for the Trees

Y'all. It's easy to feel like you're playing Whac-A-Mole with crises, even in the somewhat calmer days. In the past year, I've been angry about: abortion access, trans rights, book bans, assholes denying the results of elections, journalists being threatened, uncompensated labor at universities, too many tests and not enough recess at my kid's school, parents who think cops and Jesus belong in public schools, that our mayor wants to involuntarily commit unhoused folks and abolish 3K and cut funding to libraries (and he's a *Democrat!*), that someone else's mayor voted to allow drones to assassinate their civilians, that the World Cup was played on stadiums build with migrant blood. And a million other things. Oof. Looking at this list, it's easy to see that the world is on fire, which leads to decision paralysis. If I try to fix everything, I'm bobbing and weaving into issues I know almost nothing about, let along getting a grasp on who *is* organizing around these issues, and getting burned out when I don't see change.

What do you do? If you're like me and you're a magpie for issues—if you see them as all interconnected in this struggle for freedom, and you have friends embedded at different places, you take stock of your resources. Money here, time there, writing here, talking about it all on social media and in person. I am a writer, it's what I do, and so I can write about a good number of things if there are experts willing to help me understand what's going on. You can show solidarity in different ways without it defining you—or trying to co-opt momentum from folks who have made a specific issue their lives.

Learning from the past

It's easy to get overwhelmed and exhausted by the scope of what needs to be done.

As the Resistance struggled to keep fascism at bay, organizers were often overwhelmed with how much there was to do: keeping draconian policies from passing, challenging the legislation that did pass both in the courts and on the streets, and ensuring that democratically elected officials felt the pressure to resist as well. When I asked folks from Indivisible about the problems and struggles in American politics, I repeatedly heard the same types of responses. Gerrymandering. *Citizens United.* [📢] Voter suppression. The media. Although there wasn't a sustained institutional critique, there was a sense that something was wrong with our voting apparatus that made it difficult to affect change. People agreed that money needed to be kept out of politics. They were gravely concerned about gerrymandering (and, with good reason, it seems, after the 2019 SCOTUS decision that said courts could do literally nothing about partisan gerrymandering).[28] These issues—money in politics, voter suppression, partisan gerrymandering—were the roots of a broken system.

The question, then, becomes how to focus: how to avoid the inevitable burnout that comes when you feel like the world is on fire and you have to put out all of the flames at once. And that's really hard.

Don't Mobilize over People

As you look at the world, allow yourself to get angry, decide to change, and start to figure out how; it's so easy to assume that things are *so* broken that no one has ever tried to fix it. There is so much that you don't know, and that you don't know you don't know (this is sounding a lot like Donald Rumsfeld, Bush's secretary of defense, when he blathered on about known knowns and unknown unknowns . . . but there's some truth).[29] When you get angry about something, don't let that anger blind you to curiosity about why things are true—and those causes are so important for making change, and knowing what other people are doing as well to address the issue. There *are* people working in the space that you're passionate about—find them.

When I was teaching, I did a lot of career counseling of students who wanted to change the world. And inevitably, when we'd sit down to talk about what they wanted to do, they'd say something like "I am going to start an NGO to teach children in Africa to read," one student told me. "How do you know that these don't already exist?" I replied. "We'd see it on the news if they existed," they told me. "The media has such a liberal bias they'd be all over that shit." Hmmm . . .

Look. Before you think you're the person to solve a problem, and start sucking up resources, see what other people are doing. Part of this is also getting smarter—emotionally and intellectually—without relying on people to do the emotional labor of educating you.

Learning from the past

Obviously, there is a sense that people only decide to engage when it is convenient for them—but there's also a sense that they'll leave when it gets hard, or when the issue doesn't matter. As people, we need to play the long game to study the issues, learn the history, and convey to people that we are in it for the long game.

When community groups tried to reach out to newly organized Indivisible groups, they encountered resistance in part because the newly mobilizing resistance often wouldn't see the overlap between their work and the country's problematic past—they couldn't see how many people had been in the organizing space for generations. As Tanisha told me: "I went to a meeting when Trump first got elected, there had to be about 15 new organizations in that room. And yeah, my response is like, 'Really?' Like so Black people, Indigenous people and Brown people are dealing with this shit since Columbus's ass got lost. And so now y'all thinking 'Oh my God, what about me?' And I said, 'This is not even about you.' I said, I'm gonna tell y'all, when White people get a cold, we get pneumonia."[30]

In 2017, when the millions of Americans like me woke up to find themselves in an impossible world and wanted to do something, sometimes it was hard to envision how to fit new folks into old organizing structures. Even as people wanted the groups to grow, it was sometimes difficult to cede ground to newcomers: Organizers had mixed emotions when it came to recruiting new people into the fold. Who gets to claim the title of activist? There was some tension between new members of organizations and old, in terms of who got to adopt the mantle of organizer (and what work earned you that label; one long-time organizer lamented: "These days, someone who attends only one of our meetings will call themselves an organizer. I've spent my whole life effectively trying to cajole my fellow citizens into taking ownership and building power. I don't call myself an organizer and they do)."

This might sound hard, because there are so many people who, at various times, are eager to change the world—why would we stop that? I particularly loved, without really thinking too hard about it, interviews with feisty old White women who were determined to save the world. I loved these interviews. At one point my brother Ben, who helped me conduct these interviews, called me and said, "I think old people might just save the world after all." Of course, it's reminiscent of the oft-attributed (but hard to pin down the original) Gloria Steinem quote: "Women get more radical as they age. One day an army of gray-haired women may quietly take over the Earth." What a lovely, redemptive image.

But then, I interviewed Rosa, a young Black woman in a majority-Black southern city. Rosa runs an organization of community empowerment that was suddenly taken over by people after the election. Old White women had shown up and immediately started to take up space.

> It's almost like there's a fight when everybody's working for the same thing. White women are like "why are you fighting me, like all I'm trying to do is fight for your cause," and we are like, "but if you knew what my cause was, you would be willing to let me speak" These women were showing up and sucking all of the air out of the organizing that younger women of color were participating in.

People need to learn how *not* to do this: how to learn from, be curious about, be supportive of, the work Black people are doing. Indeed, as one White activist involved in organizing in the city of Philadelphia told me, there was a huge problem of not understanding the work being done in the Black community: "In a city like Philly, which is predominantly African American, I'm only now realizing that there are parallel tracks for people are redoing everything that the Black people have already been trying to do . . . we didn't know." [🔊] How do you avoid this? How do you make sure you're not strangling resources from the communities that *are* doing the work—how can you instead ask them what they need? Money? Allyship? A parallel group doing work in White communities? The answer probably changes from case to case, but thinking about how this work can happen synergistically matters. One way is to find the progressive coalition in your state and figure out what they're doing and how you can help.

One protester from the Bay Area tried to infuse Indivisible with this sense of allyship by pairing his Indivisible chapter with Standing Up for Racial Justice (SURJ) to get people to talk about race. He told me about wanting to make that transition and to "Shift from Indivisible to SURJ—and that appealed to me 'cause it's led by a very powerful Black woman, and I can really learn from her leadership, and just be an ally." But people wouldn't attend SURJ meetings, and he felt like nothing was really changing: "I keep seeing these same patterns play out, sort of supremacy in the way we organize and the way we think, so I'm not particularly optimistic long term." This unwillingness for people to interrogate their own communities, their own practices is a real example of NIMBYism (and this was in San Francisco, where they then killed the housing bill. So, the "progressives" don't really have a critique of neoliberalism, do they?).

Part of being willing to be pushed to a more encompassing sense of social justice is realizing that what you think is progressive may actually not be, and it's worth having an open mind—getting smarter, developing your analysis, being open to learning from people who are smarter than you.

The Power of Yes, and . . .

If you've ever taken an improv class, you probably know about the "yes, and . . ." rule. The idea is simple: Someone starts a scene, and your job is to say "yes" to whatever they've developed, and then add the "and." So person one shows up at a store holding a cage with a parrot in it. Person two doesn't say "That's not a parrot, that's a dinosaur!" Instead they say "Thank you very much for coming to the bank today," (the yes) "but I'm afraid I can't help you." "Why not?" person one demands. The audience assumes that it's because they are at a bank, which isn't a place for animals. "Because," person two replies, "your parrot is dead." And the audience roars with laughter.

I may not be the next inductee into the Screenwriters' Guild, but I have a point here: The world would be better if we learned to say "yes, and" a little more often. Yes, that person is problematic, and maybe we can work together on this one thing. Yes, it's great that an unprecedented number of White women are mobilizing, *and* they need to take leadership from Black women. Yes, governments are evil and people who live under those governments can be good. The power to think about things in complexities, to hold two ideas as true in your mind, will save us from a lot of the knee-jerk reactions and hot takes of the moment. We need to dream of a different future, while also working to make the world we live in better with the tools we have at our disposal.

I think about the Obama administration's immigration policy a lot in terms of the need to hold more than one idea in your mind at once. Obama earned the name "deporter-in-chief" from critics of his administration's decision to deport more people than any other administration (of course, his successor beat that record).[31] At the same time, when Congress refused to act on protecting the rights of people brought to this country as children, Obama signed an executive order called Deferred Action and Adjudication (DACA), allowing "Dreamers" (kiddos brought to the US as children) to stay in the country, live, and work without risk of deportation. And Jose Ramos, the influential journalist for Univision, mused that the symbolism of the Obama presidency was enormously important for immigrant children across the country:

> The very fact that Barack Obama—the son of an immigrant—became president leaves Latinos with hope

that a Latino could also be president one day . . . Obama became the first African American president in a country with a history of slavery, racism, and discrimination. I don't see why we cannot do exactly the same . . . I am absolutely convinced that the first Latino or Latina president has already been born. Juan in Los Angeles or Pedro in Miami or Sofia in New York . . . He did it. We can do it, too.[32]

Learning from the past

The politics surrounding the Women's March, and the other major marches of the time, are *complicated*. Women of color who talked with me critiqued the organizations for failing to be substantively inclusive. Rosa expressed frustration with the Women's March, saying that "there were supposed to be spaces for women for color, but all of those spaces were manipulated and controlled by the machine of privileged women that took over."

Along with the pushback against the Women's March, there was resistance to March For Our Lives, the post-Parkland march: [📢]

> Here's the deal about March For Our Lives . . . there were too many police. My Black people are not coming out for that. Cause we don't have that relationship with the police like you do. I said, "So the amount of police that you thought were safe for the kids is unsafe for Black people." It's having those hard conversations with people that want to be allies and say, you need to take leadership and have us at the table every time you want to even organize something, even if we might not come. They're like, "Why can't we get out more Black kids?" Because you had a bunch of police there. The same police that harass these kids daily.

In real terms, what does this mean? It likely means denying police forces the platform for copaganda and standing in solidarity with the

Black community, and rejecting "blue washing" of your movement. It means critically analyzing *why* organizing spaces are all White, and findings ones that aren't. Being a better ally means listening to critiques of power.

In Sum: Pressure and Protest Work

Here's something sobering. You know all of those book bans across the country, pulling Judy Blume and books with LGBTQ characters out of the hands of students? Do you know how many people are behind those petitions? Eleven. Sixty percent of the book challenges were filed by 11 people. One woman who has committed to challenging a book a week is getting national profiles right now. If those 11 ignorant yo-yos can have that kind of impact on the world, what can you and your ten besties do?[33] You can probably save the books.

And it's not just that I'm telling you this is true. In 2023, it leaked that Scholastic, our favorite book fair fairy, had taken all of the books "about diversity" (read: that had a character with brown skin or a non-cis-het family), and put them into a segregated catalog that schools had to *opt in to*. This included books like a biography of Supreme Court Justice Ketanji Brown Jackson (where would they have shelved such a book about Clarence Thomas? The mind boggles). But when people found out about it, they protested—they contacted their administrations and PTOs and wrote editorials and got in touch with Scholastic directly . . . and Scholastic apologized and desegregated its catalog.

The fact is protest works. It changes public opinion, it has an impact on policy, it convinces more people to organize. And the protest that works has our three main ingredients. As you mobilize, make sure it follows the CSI:

Constant—As you build organizations and figure out your mobilization strategy, reflect on how this will become integrated into your life.

Slow—In this chapter we talked about having a blueprint for action and learning from the past is critical to mounting an effective resistance.

Inclusive—Being inclusive means both acknowledging that there are people in the world who are already doing this work, and learning from the action they have taken that is effective or ineffective, as well as pushing your allies to the left and ensuring that they are also embracing a vision of change.

Step Four:

SUSTAIN YOUR MOMENTUM

I think political activism needs to be very local right now . . . and this is not something that Americans do.

—AN IMMIGRATION ACTIVIST FROM TEXAS, 2018

In 2014, two years out from the 2016 elections. I was happily living in Somerville, Massachusetts. My son, as he learned to talk, picked up a few words of Portuguese from our Brazilian neighbors. I was finishing my dissertation at Rutgers, which had just been recognized for graduating the largest number of Black undergraduate students in the country. Although I didn't know it, within a year we'd see Obergefell pass. I was in love with the Obamas, and excited about his successors and continuing the progressive work of the past few years. I didn't quite think that we were in a post-racial, post-gender-politics society, but I thought we were close. You all know how this story ends. I was wrong.

As we know now, this privilege served as a double bubble, first against realizing that not all of White America was thinking like me, and second that not all of Black and Brown America was as safe and successful as the folks in the bubble I had created around me.

DISPATCHES FROM THE FIELD 12:
MEET CLEMENTINE

Clementine is a protester from the Pacific Northwest who was a major part of the Reclaim Idaho movement. Here is her story:

I'm 47, I have two teenage daughters, I've been married for more than 20 years. I was always politically aware. I'm college educated, I'm a professional. I didn't think I had the time or the inclination to get involved in anything political other than screaming with my friends on Facebook when something pissed us off. The election galvanized me. My daughter was 11. I watched her turn to a friend a few days before the election and grabbed her friend's arm and said very excitedly, "Our next president is going to be a woman."

And I was thrilled and then a few days later I was absolutely, completely in tears. It took me a couple of months to sort of really acknowledge this is really happening. I truly believed until the inauguration that there was going to be some Deus ex machina and we were going to get out of this shit show.

Then I realized, if I want a country here for my daughters and my grandchildren, I need to get off my ass, get on the phone, knock on doors, send that four millionth email, organize.... Because I don't trust the Democrats in my county, I've gathered women I can trust and I said, 'We are the shadow cabinet in this county, and we are gonna get out the vote.'"

When I earned my PhD and we moved all the way to the middle of the country so I could work at a small liberal arts school that looked a little like Hogwarts, our first visitor was Sebastian, one of the friends I had made when I was studying in Germany. The moving company had lost all of our things, and we were all camping out in our rental house: my husband, my 18-month-old son, and our very flexible European visitor. We bought lawn chairs at Target. That night, we picked up takeout (there was no Grub Hub or Uber Eats in 2015 Nebraska, we learned), and we perched my computer on the kitchen counter, streaming the Republican primary debates and drinking prosecco with our Chinese food. Donald Trump started speaking, and Sebastian grew quiet, watching. "He will win," Sebastian declared, "he will become president." Jim and I pushed back, but Sebastian was certain. "We saw it happen in Germany; it's been brewing here." I've thought a lot about that moment in the years since then. The Overton Window hadn't yet shifted to the possibility of Trump being the nominee (remember Jeb?) let alone the most likely candidate for president. And yet my friends from outside the country could read the landscape clearly, see his path to victory, even when I couldn't.

This chapter is all about tending to your community.[1] As we've moved through the book, you have found your people; you've come up with mobilizing strategies that fit your life and feel good. Now it's time to make sure that your mobilization and your advocacy do two things: makes your community a better, healthier place to be, and that they enable you to care for the members in your group. You can take whatever issue is motivating you, and use it to think about how to focus on making your community better. As one person put it to me: "Trump is 95 percent evil and 5 percent positive because he's awoken Democrats to the importance of local politics, reinvigorating the party with new ideas."

Local activism needs to be a form of love, a way of protecting your fellow activists and the community as you dream about what can be better. As an organizer from Texas told me: "You have to organize locally if you're going to protect each other, to fight for your country and to continue to fight for the Constitution, for the laws that you believe in—there's the small optimism that is always at its core." To me, optimism (and a belief that things *don't* need to look the way that they do) is at the core of why I wrote this book, why people do the work they do.

It's also *necessary* that people who are interested in preserving democracy become more agile in thinking locally. When Biden won, Democrats breathed a sigh of relief, but then Republicans were able to pivot to small and local—pouring their energy into Moms for Liberty and school boards (and Democrats pushed back! And kicked Moms for Liberty out of schools—not everywhere, but in a lot of places!). In this way, building community is both the problem and the solution to democracy. It's the solution, because at the end of the day *all* change needs to be local. If you're focusing nationally, they'll come for your schools. If you're focusing on the state level, they'll come for your city. Movements that aren't in and of their community, that aren't fundamentally local, don't survive because they don't have the community members to give them energy.

Even so, communitarianism—being small for the sake of being small—isn't the only, or the best solution. Violence comes from within communities. The people who are following protesters around with assault rifles are often just from the suburbs down the road. Communities can be protective, and they can at times feel stifling. They can reject the values of inclusion and multiracial/anti-patriarchal organizing in the name of keeping the community "safe"—misguided utilitarian values meets racist ideas about who the ideal community members are. You only have to look at the NIMBY approach to everything from affordable housing to zoning regulations to see that values can be flexible in a community, and progressive communities can quickly turn conservative.

Building *chosen* and intentional community is the only real solution. If you want to fight where you are, great. But, if where you are is toxic and you need a chosen community to nurture you, go find those people and fight there instead. But those of us with privilege have the obligation to spend it to work on our communities to change. Remember—once you learn who is already on the ground (Step One) and what is already happening in your community (Step Two), you can start working toward systemic community change.

DISPATCHES FROM THE FIELD 13:
ORGANIZING FOR MEDICAID EXPANSION IN DEEP RED AMERICA

Now I want to tell you the story of a little organization called Reclaim Idaho. Even as the battle to save the ACA was raging at the national level, there were local efforts to expand and preserve health care coverage as well. I was fortunate to talk to two organizers who had been on the ground collecting signatures for Medicaid expansion in Idaho. These were some of my favorite interviews because it really encapsulated for me what community organizing can accomplish, even in deeply red areas.

What happens in places where political competition has been eliminated? One protester from Reclaim Idaho told me: "Indivisible is about calling your senators, calling Congress members—well they don't give two shits. They literally don't care . . . I mean, it's a joke. You get a letter back from Jim Risch that doesn't even reference what you emailed him about." So, they focused on Medicaid expansion.

To set the scene: In Idaho, getting an initiative on the ballot is a tricky math problem: you have to collect signatures from 6 percent of registered voters in half of the counties in Idaho. And this has to be done by April 30—so during the coldest, snowiest, most miserable seasons in Idaho, in a state that is immensely large geographically. (In the summer of 2017, I attended a rally in Idaho Falls for Families Belong Together. I talked to one of my participants while I was there—"you're only 10 hours away from me!" she quipped. Idaho is huge.)

It became clear early on that a ballot initiative was the only way to expand Medicaid in the state: a state representative told one organizer: "We will never sign off on anything that has Obama's name on it." That was their reasoning for letting people die in our state." Another organizer told me her representative was on record as saying: "No one dies from lack of access to health care." Their mission was clear—now they had to find the signatures.

Reclaim Idaho began to organize the campaign. And so they knocked on doors. In the snow and the rain, for months. One organizer told me: "We were required to get 56,192 signatures. That number is burned into my brain. We collected well over 100,000 signatures, and 73,000 were validated. We qualified 21 districts, not just 18." In November, 61 percent of voters approved the initiative (in Utah, 53 percent of voters approved a measure, and in Nebraska 54 percent of voters approved, so Idaho's results were seriously impressive).

Activists in Idaho felt like the big tent of the Democratic Party didn't have a lot of room for organizers like them: "Idahoans . . . we're painted as red, but we're far more Libertarian than red . . . we joke that we're libertarian Democrats: 'Hey, it's none of my business what the hell you do . . .'" Trying to explain what a western Democrat is to people back East. It's very difficult to explain why the Second Amendment doesn't need to be repealed . . ." They used the organizing structure of Medicaid expansion to strategically increase support for blue candidates, and piggybacked to get progressives elected.

Here's how one activist targeted her messaging in Idaho.

I tell everyone—don't talk about the moral issue, don't talk about the right thing to do, talk about the money. Montana is very similar to Idaho. They saved $30 million the first year they expanded Medicaid . . . remind people we're already paying for it. Our tax dollars are already going into the pool. How about we pay for it for people in Idaho.

In organizing in this environment, it's finding those nonpartisan issues, like health care being a human right. You shouldn't lose your home because you got cancer. It's just not an even trade. Explaining to people what Medicaid expansion does for us tax-wise in the state—those are really nonpartisan issues. Republicans love it when we spend less money. I center a lot of my conversation, and organization, and outreach around the conservative math that comes with it before we even get to the social issue or the humanitarian issue. Showing the math before ideology makes it a nonpartisan issue. With our taxes, we've already paid for it—we don't want to keep spending twice. That has brought volunteers out of the woodwork. Those who started out to be in support of it because of fiscal reasons are now meeting others who need it because they're hard-working families.

In the end, Reclaim Idaho won the battle to get Medicaid expansion on the ballot, and it passed in 2018 with 61 percent of the vote. The legislature responded by making it even harder to bring ballot initiatives to the ballot, and the courts intervened to kill an initiative to raise money for public schools in the state.

Do this . . .

Here are five ways to embed your movement in your community, with lessons from activists about what worked.

This chapter's list of dos:

1. Think of local organizing strategies.
2. Show up where the government isn't.
3. Push your community where you want it to be.
4. Find your people, even in hostile places.
5. Embrace different time horizons.

Local Organizing as Strategy

If you're new to organizing, one step is to figure out what's going on at the very most local level. What's your school board up to these days? Your city council? Are there any groups doing exciting things for fair housing or gender inclusion in your town? Chances are, something cool is happening somewhere—find it, join their Facebook page, and get involved. Seeing real work accomplished in your community is important and galvanizing. The flipside is true as well—if bad work is being done, maybe it's time to counterbalance.

The most effective pressure campaigns work on multiple levels. Yes, it's important to get national attention on issues, but it's equally important to talk to city council members and county commissioners and school boards. Yes, it's important to turn out on a national day of action, but it's equally important to show up in solidarity if abortion clinics in your town are being picketed or if local neighborhoods are being targeted for gentrification.

These local organizing strategies often work so well because they lend themselves to setting SMART goals (specific, measurable, attainable, realistic, timely). It might take a generation to get an unjust law overturned by the Supreme Court, but only a year to get city council to pay attention. Local issues tend to be tangible.

Learning from what worked

One of the under-told stories of our time is the effort activists put into reimagining their local communities. An immigration activist spoke to me about the Resistance against ICE in 2018. In our conversation, she emphasized that focusing on local activism—on every level—was key to systemic resistance: "Now even airlines are saying 'we will not deport children.' This matters . . . you don't have to do everything that you're being told to do, and we need resistance movements on every single level to say: 'We can't do this.'"

Here's what people told me worked to organize on a local level to sustain the momentum of a group. Many of these groups had massive Facebook groups and mailing lists and often turned out 200 to 300 people at smaller rallies and tens of thousands at large marches. How do you navigate groups that big? How do you get people to keep showing up for meetings and simultaneously attract new people? One activist from the Northeast, who is married to a clergy member, observed: "New people need to be welcomed. In a church, if you don't have seven new friends in a year, you'll leave the church." Creating that sense of community and connection was a major focus of these groups' organizational work.

When national attention fades, local groups can either fade away or step up and begin getting real work done. After the 2018 election, groups continued the rallies—Indivisible Seattle had weekly Tuesday rallies, and Indivisible Houston only missed their weekly rallies for Hurricane Harvey. Rallies, however, are useful for a show of force: using bodies to publicly demonstrate. To be sure, this is a book about *slow* organizing. We can't keep the dial turned up all the time. However, when the moment of outrage has passed, organizers often struggle with how to keep people motivated and engaged. As one organizer lamented: "Meetings are getting smaller as people get less resist-oriented and more wait-it-out oriented." Another organizer told me that the ethos of the group changed when they stopped holding regular rallies: "The energy just kind of evaporated. It let a lot of air out of the balloon." Given the need for connection, how can ritual and routine sustain a group even while making room for downtime?

Here are four ways to keep energy levels high and engaged.

1. Set achievable goals. Successful groups created direct, achievable goals for their organization. For instance, some groups decide to dedicate Wednesdays to showing solidarity with other groups, whether through canvassing or fundraising. Other groups end each meeting with marching orders—call these people, show up for this action, and be ready to talk about this issue. There was always a sense of moving forward. A member of a California group put it this way:

> Our group never fell apart is because we always had small, manageable goals you could work on and be successful every time. These sorts of things helped keep me sane and also helped keep us organized. Fatigue when you're organizing on a grassroots level is really common and I think when you get large, large groups, you start getting this feeling like 'oh, it doesn't matter if I show up.' When you have every person functioning toward something, I think you're more likely to have people turn out

One victory a week, a SMART goal, helped them avoid feeling like they would never accomplish anything, and kept people feel motivated to keep showing up.

2. Pivot to the local level. Another group described the pivot to local elections as the way they managed to keep momentum: "Trump fatigue is real—local and statewide election pivot reinvigorated people who are just exhausted—statewide pivot gave people space to organize around what interested them most." Focusing attention on local elections is a way to make real change—indeed, local, communal work, whether on elections or in the community, is key to accomplishing tangible things with differences you can see.

3. Find battles that can be won. These stories were signs of a newly awakened sense of civic engagement, though it was unclear if the activism could be sustained. Many other activists told me about channeling their energy into local projects—not just harm reduction but ways to make their community *well*—to help it thrive. For example, one activist from the mid-Atlantic described all the anger and frustration he felt after the 2016 election. He and his fiancé joined a local Indivisible chapter but felt the group was ineffectual. In the meantime, they learned that a gas station would be opening on their block, adding traffic and pollution to their neighborhood. The story has a very *Parks and Rec* feeling: a gas station was going to be built in their neighborhood, and the community wanted a park instead. "I really channeled a lot of my frustration and anger with national politics with this local issue," he told me. The neighborhood group protested, testified; they learned zoning laws, met with City Council . . . and ultimately they won! As he told me, "One hundred percent success would mean that this land would have been used solely as a green space. Ninety percent success would have been a mix of cool commerce with a green space. Right now, they're talking about either a bank or fast food . . . It's not what we want, but it's better than a gas station." By preventing a gas station from being built, this organizer helped change the landscape of his community—and staved off his feeling of hopelessness.

4. Realize some struggles are systemic. Voting, postcard campaigns, rallies, and resisting gas stations are all material, short-term goals. Not every community problem is like that. Systems and structures matter. Kat, an activist from Texas, told me:

> Serving folks that are marginalized or underserved will, by default, benefit the rest of my community. Until the marginalized drug user who's homeless and stigmatized at every turn, has rights, then how can I fully say that I have my rights . . . in Texas, there's a lot to fight for. I'm not from Texas; I chose to be here. And I struggle with whether

my time would be better spent in a place where the death penalty isn't given out so frivolously, and where abortion is legal and accepted, or where harm reduction is legal or accepted, and at the end of the day, I chose to fight my fight here and see if I can change that.

DISPATCHES FROM THE FIELD 14:
MEET THELMA

Thelma is a lifelong organizer who played a major role in Reclaim Philadelphia. Her story shows that local organizing, even in big cities, can have a major impact on politics.

I became much more aware, I guess, one could say. This was very interesting because I'd gone to Berkeley as an undergrad and I wasn't anybody who ever protested; never did anything. But then I come back and then I actually get quite politicized really, because I really feel that George W. Bush is so horrifyingly stupid and lying to get us into a war. I was one of those people who lost a lot of friends right at the beginning because I followed the Union of Concerned Scientists. You're too young probably to remember this, but there was a lot of lying going on that a lot of people who were paying attention the country just followed it. That was where I began to get very agitated about what was happening. Then in my recent life, I started to do electoral campaigning. I've done 19 election cycles. I'm known as what's called a super volunteer. I'm talking like I was volunteering at the end of every one of those elections like 40 hours a week or more. At the end of the Bernie campaign here in South Philadelphia where I now live, about 30 of us set up a group called Reclaim Philadelphia to have a progressive society that we could all live in.

Many of those people are also Democratic Socialist party members. They are very active in electoral politics. We've done a lot of actions to stand in solidarity with other people who are in need. There are labor unions and we got contacted, for example, by the Dakota Access Pipeline people so we shut down a bank along with several other groups one day. We've done marches. Right at the beginning, the first thing we did was deal with the Bernie situation. Hillary was there and there was going . . . They were gonna be right here in the city and so our first action ever was actually to have the Democratic National Committee (DNC) come forward with who was donating money to support the DNC. We knew that the host committee was our ex-governor, ex-mayor now . . . and that's a Democrat who was now a lobbyist for the fracking industry, which is Ed Rendell. Then we also had the number two at Comcast and the number one at Pennsylvania Blue Cross Blue Shield. Some huge Republican supports that had worked against socialized health care against Obamacare. They're the host committee for Hillary. It was just so galling. We wrote an editorial that got published in The New York Times. We had stories that were picked up on NPR nationwide. We also went to their individual offices and to their individual homes demanding that they release the information so that we could call attention to the fact that the Democratic National Convention was being supported by Republicans in large part. We made some inroads there. We can't say it wasn't a success. For our first effort ever, we were very happy.

We also started a bunch of training. Reclaim Philadelphia comes from within the activist community. The group has trained other people in small weekend events. We've also gone and met for other training with other groups in the northeast region. It's very much an emphasis in Reclaim. It's very much on electoral politics, but it is also based in a notion of solidarity, so the fact that the right was much more organized than the left is the left needs to be more organized. There's a lot of people from the leadership that go and work with other groups, with Indivisible, with various groups in Pennsylvania, so that they'll step up for us. It's a very . . . very much an idea of knitting together as much as possible.

The basic thing, however, is an idea of knowing your neighbors. We actually have people go and knock on every door in their neighborhood to tell them that they're from Reclaim, to tell them that we have a different vision. What are they happy with, not happy with in city, state, national politics. It gives the people a chance to vent. We did all this and as a result of the fact that we had already been on so many doors, we've added 220 people in an alliance of progressive Democrats. We ran 220 people for committeeperson, which in Philadelphia's the lowest level of a very big Democratic machine. We won 186 of those. Now we're starting a progressive caucus.

Show up Where the Government Isn't

As a member of your community, you know where government is working—and where it isn't. Even though I am ideologically pretty far left of center compared to the rest of the United States, I suspect that I may feel centrist to some of you, my lovely readers—at least I hope there are some of you frustrated that the book is too moderate and prosaic, because it means that there are visionaries out there imagining a more optimistic future.

Although I believe in progressive government—that government can do good things if it has good people, sufficiently pressured and motivated, I also fully believe that we need to be willing to show up where government isn't. We should make demands on the government to provide resources, and then we should do it ourselves when they don't. Part of organizing is being the change we want to see in our communities—not just insisting the government do things for us.

During the pandemic, state governments in the conservative states I was living in (Nebraska, then Texas), were *not* meeting what I needed in terms of providing a safe, accessible education for my son. Online learning did not work for him. I had no faith in the COVID precautions the schools were taking, particularly with my new baby and my high-risk family members. So, we homeschooled for a year and a half. Parts of it were *amazing*. We were in a pod with close friends, and Sorin learned about biomes and Frida Kahlo and went on nature quests and jumped on trampolines. It really resonated with my theory of what education *should be*. And given world enough, money enough, and time, maybe we would have stuck with it (or maybe started a school). Instead, we moved to New York, where the government *was* providing what we thought was a safe learning environment, and we enrolled our kids back into public school. But the freedom of homeschooling stuck with me—the ability to opt out of governmental services that aren't serving your needs, and to do your own thing. For me, this was only possible *because* there was community, in the form of local homeschooling communities and online communities, that provided the support and resources I needed to make it happen.

I know that these conversations get weird sometimes, because any conversation about resources and public expenditures is fraught.[2] To be clear, I am advocating a vision of socialist democracy where we deeply fund cities and communities: parks, playgrounds, libraries, schools, healthcare, artists. Public money should be for *all* of us (and there's a rich history of defunding public goods once it isn't just for White people—just check out the history of community swimming pools).[3] We should fund public enterprises—and then when they aren't funded, we should be prepared to engage in mutual aid, helping each other. But sometimes, instead of participating in a system that is failing you, it's okay to exit for a little while.[4]

DISPATCHES FROM THE FIELD 15:
MEET MORGAN

Morgan is an activist from the Northeast focused on trans and disability rights. This is their story.

Yeah. Let's see. I grew up in a small town 90 percent white, pretty upper-middle class. When I was growing up, I was raised in a Unitarian Universalist congregation from an old UU family on my mom's side. There was a lot of general liberalism, I guess, I would say in the church around taking action for human rights and those kinds of things. I didn't really see my family or many people I knew well in the congregation doing direct activism work, but I did get instilled with some values around, like, showing up for other people, at least in a theoretical sense.

When I was in high school, I did a program called The Food Project, which brings together young people from all over the Boston area, in the city, suburbs, all different backgrounds. That helped me understand that I could make a change in the world and even if I was 16. That started me doing different kinds of food justice work and having more awareness of the world. I still hadn't deepened my political knowledge and awareness. That happened. I went for a year abroad when I studied in India. I came back and readjusting to US culture helped me really realize more about race and gender than I had before within our own culture, readjusting.

I was like, "Oh, yeah, Whiteness is a thing that has a culture and its own way of behaving and doing things." I experienced some pretty hard things when I was living in India and coming back and readjusting also meant recalibrating in a world where I knew that really crappy things could happen to me and at the same time recovering from trauma on one end while also having the opportunity to take action on the worlds around me at the same time, and my whole awareness about the world around me growing so much deeper politically. That combination was really powerful for me and definitely helped catalyze me as someone who does radical and progressive organizing work. That was in 2011, and since then I think my perspective on what activism is and what taking action for justice looks really different in a lot of different ways, and I've found my own paths and ways for that. That's my origin story.

Coming back from my time in India I also started having more mental and physical health issues, and so I was navigating chronic illness throughout most of my 20s. I still am. Balancing that with traditional organizing work, showed me that it really wasn't sustainable, and it isn't for a lot of people. I didn't for a while. For a while I didn't think of myself as disabled. I thought I was having a hard time doing things and I was sick for a little while. Over time and with the help of friends who do disability justice work, I started to have a new framework of activism. At the same time, I also was learning how to do social justice education and peer mediation, and a few years ago started writing for Everyday Feminism about nonbinary issues. Pretty much that was the first time anyone had written on a national stage, I think, and had gotten a lot of traction about nonbinary stuff. That's one of the first times. I started to see my own path and space in this movement work as someone who does education and writing and helps other people learn and grow around it. I realized pretty quickly that doing direct organizing work was going to be too very traumatizing and also too physically draining for me, but the education work was something where I have both the skill and excitement.

Unfortunately, also around that time about three years ago, four years ago, is when I came out as trans. I was really vulnerable and ended up getting into an abusive relationship with someone. My organizing again was re-colored by realizing how much our movements ignore survivors and don't support them and so I would say that a lot of being pushed out of different movement spaces for different reasons, disability, being a survivor, being trans in different ways, have shaped what I end up doing as what's left, but I also have built a really strong career in the work that I do, and now I do youth organizing work on a global platform for a living. I'm going to get back into writing again soon. I don't live in [that area] anymore, so I can go to organizing events without worrying about running into my rapist. I've definitely become more cynical, yeah, I would say more cynical about humanity, but also the people that you think are supposed to be there for you or theoretically on your side. They really aren't necessarily at all. I've come to expect shitty behavior from any type of person, and I think a lot of leftist-type people organizing in a more mainstream way think that the movement is infallible or something, and for me the movement has hurt me as much as if not more than outside forces.

That movement could mean a lot of things. It could be an activist space; it could mean queer community in general. What I'm left with is the actual work that I do, which is developing youth leaders and spirituality and building community and care spaces, I'm really good at and I love to do, but I also, the different intersections of my identity mean that I'm really isolated.

Learning from what worked

1. Don't wait for the government to save you. An activist affiliated with the Democratic Socialists of America told me about how the DSA passed out more masks than the government of San Francisco in response to the forest fires, starting by giving them to all of the unhoused people they could find. They didn't call their representatives, they didn't petition, they distributed masks: "We can manifest the world we want to see," he insisted.[5]

2. Rebuild communities where people can be well. Indeed, during times of tragedy, it's been activists, not the government, who have shown up repeatedly on the local level. As one organizer from the South told me in 2018:

> During Hurricane Katrina, there were more boots on the ground in New Orleans than there were Nazi boots on the ground in Paris during the occupation during WWII. And now people have rebuilt their city, and it's incredible. It's not perfect, it's one of the most challenged, screwed-up cities in America, but it's incredible—I think it's my favorite city in the world. It's like we've seen in Gaza, people are willing to charge the fence. When the Berlin Wall came down, there is this pivotal moment, when people charge the fence. And I keep asking myself, would Americans ever charge the fence? If there is going to be a successful movement, we have to start teaching people about local engagement and really becoming invested and realizing not just that it could happen here, but it is happening here.

Part of charging the fence means caring for those who are on the frontlines. Mental health is a ubiquitous concept, one that is too complex to fully tackle in this book. But part of the goal is to create communities where people can be psychologically, physically, emotionally well. Particularly in red states, community work is often what can be done without legislative victories; as Kat mused in one of our conversations: "There are just so many losses within these fields of activism—even if I can't help people get good legislation passed, maybe I can make their day a little brighter. I can give somebody who doesn't have clean socks clean socks." She paused. "I keep hoping I can make people see pregnant people as whole entire people."

Push Your Community to Where You Want It to Be

On a cold winter day in early 2018, I visited the Museum of African American History and Culture in Washington, DC. Emilia was an infant, and she slept the whole time in a wrap on my chest. I was so worried about traveling with her, about her getting the flu.

That day, I was one of the only White people at the museum, and I relaxed into watching how my Black companions to the museum were experiencing the exhibitions. I watched and watched. I nursed my daughter in the movie about the Freedom Rides. The story of the museum is one of resistance. It is a story of economics. It was breathtaking (as others I'm sure have described more completely). To me, it was precisely the narrative I wanted to read. Slavery, racism, was an economic invention. People are always struggling for their freedom. Enslaved people have always resisted. Not just Nat Turner. Always. I watched an old, old lady, dressed in a red church outfit, approach a portrait of Martin Luther King, Jr. She touched his face. "That boy," she whispered.

I entered the room with Emmitt Till's casket. No photos are allowed in there. It's a sacred space. You hear the voice of Emmitt's mother. Tears streamed down my face as I listened. I kissed my baby girl's head and imagined the work it will take to make our community, our nation, worthy of this sacrifice.

Just like you need to imagine ways for your allies to move left, you need to do the same for your community. Envision a community where everyone can be well, and has dignity, and then reverse engineer your activism to achieve that. Community-based activism matters and works because issues are necessarily not tied to election cycles. For example, activists of color always returned to the perennial work of educating people as labor that isn't tied to an election cycle. We can do the work of educating ourselves.

Your community has people who do not think like you. When do you organize around them, and when do you have tough conversations with them? There are two times I think it's worth going to the table: when you *need* them in order to fulfill a goal (if the votes or power or resources aren't on your side), and when you think there's a group of people who are softening, willing to listen to your message.[6] On an episode of Pod Save America where the hosts were discussing how to prepare for the 2024 presidential election, one of the hosts suggested ignoring your Trump loving uncle—he's not changing—and instead focusing on your Biden-skeptical cousin. And I think that logic holds for where there's the most room for persuasion on a variety of issues.

When I started teaching in Lincoln, our department was *extremely* White, both in terms of the student body and the faculty. I had complicated feelings about teaching classes on racial politics and community organizing as a White woman at a predominantly White institution, especially when I had taught at such diverse places earlier in my career. (I wrote about this with my friend and colleague Kelly Bauer in 2018.) I put my attention into building a department where Black and Brown and queer kids could see themselves and be at home in, and I realized, with the help of some colleagues, that doing so would only work if I also saw the value in educating the White kids, many of whom had never been exposed to the study of politics and activism before.

For the first time in my adult life, I found myself in all-White classrooms, where people felt comfortable saying what was on their minds. More than one kid told me that they had never met a Black person or a Muslim person before coming to college. One student told me "I've never talked to a Black person because I don't know whether to say Black or African American." Another student agreed that talking about race isn't 'Nebraska nice,' so they just decided not to talk to Black people at all. I was . . . stunned. Ill-equipped to know how to navigate these conversations. "Well," I began, "you don't need to say Black in order to talk to someone. Ask them for help with your physics homework." Those conversations were the precursor to what would happen next. One day, a student told me, in front of an entire class, "It's okay to say f*g, but not to say ni**er, because I'm not worried about a gay person beating me up if they are offended, but a Black person is scarier and could." The whole class, as one, swiveled to look at me. After a long moment of being frozen, I said, "Well, I can see from your faces we have a lot to process. Write down what you're feeling right now, and we can return to it next time." As I read the exit slips, people split in thirds: one-third appalled, one-third uncomfortable with her language, one-third applauding her "for saying what we all think." How do you teach through that? "I just feel sad for Black people because they don't have as much as us," one student wrote.

And yet they were willing to take our classes and learn what they didn't know about the world. My goal wasn't to indoctrinate them (no matter what Turning Points USA will tell you) but instead to give them the knowledge and tools they needed to understand the world. And part of that was helping them develop a nuanced, holistic view of people they'd never encountered before. A decade earlier, I was teaching a class about post-communist transitions at Rutgers, and my normally chipper class was feeling particularly glum. "What's going on?" I asked them. One student raised her hand. "It's all just so . . . sad!" She told me. "Breadlines and starvation and no jeans and only state-approved music. What a sad way for so many people to live for so long!" And I realized that by just teaching politics, I was failing them. People aren't the systems they live inside. People who lived under communism went to movie theaters and dated and got divorced and had parties. And my students didn't know this, because how could they? So I started trying to make the world smaller for them. We read novels and watched movies and listened to podcasts and followed social media feeds of people who weren't like us so that we could feel what the world was like outside of the little part of Nebraska.

This isn't enough, because what's missing is also a sense of linked fate. In order to be convinced that our freedoms are linked, White people need to realize that they're missing something. White people can casually consume (culturally appropriate) the parts of other cultures that they find convenient. You can order in Thai on your phone, watch Beyoncé's *Homecoming* on Netflix and then watch LeBron James play basketball and never actually interact with a person of color. (After Beyoncé's 2016 Super Bowl halftime performance of "Formation" [Queen Bey!], one student told our class, "I don't think Black people should get to politicize the Super Bowl." "Is a country star singing about God and small towns not political?" I asked him.)

Learning from what worked

I didn't talk to a single person in my four years of interviews who said they had written off their neighbors; as I continued to read headlines about how out of touch we were with the rest of the United States, I saw instead a kind of funhouse mirror with progressives trying to start real conversations with conservatives in their communities, only to be rebuffed. In the meantime, the misinformation ecosystem continued to push the narrative of liberals who were out of touch with the rest of America. Here's how to keep doing the work, even if the media doesn't recognize it.

1. Find common emotional ground. One activist described using her gender and her profession as a surprise tactic to win the hearts and minds of the conservatives in her red state: "Being a construction professional and a lady welder, I get a lot of attention when I go to a jobsite. You don't see a lot of women coming out to do the decorative fireplace. It's predominantly a very conservative group, and they see my work ethic, and they see how much fun I am to be around . . . and then I start those conversations about how I feel about taxes and spending and social programs." This type of strategic positioning enabled activists to imagine talking with people across the aisle.[7]

Organizers were also highly cognizant of which frames were persuasive, especially those appealing to fiscal conservatism when talking to their red neighbors.[8] Most tried to shift the debate to a policy ground—one activist said that she spent her time trying to "get people on the right to stop talking about how Christian they are and about policy instead." By reframing the narrative, trying to suss out common ground, communities can sometimes reach a point of understanding.

2. Know when pushing won't work. As people deliberated how to address or balance the idea of talking with Republican voters, it was much more serious to them on an emotional level about issues—particularly the family separations. [📢] In 2018, one activist said "On a personal level, I've ended friendships. I don't have time for it. I'm a quarter Jewish. My father remembers the German government calling and offering reparations because they wiped out our family in the Holocaust. That, to me, is a point of responsibility as someone of Jewish heritage. If you wonder what you would've done leading up to Hitler taking power, this is it. He's treating Latino people like Hitler would."

3. Remember that democracy is local. Creating local democracy is the best way to fend off fascism. The link between democracy and local community work was so clear in the conversations I had. One activist from a red part of the Northwest noted: "Oh heck, I ignore what's going on in Washington. We've got to strengthen the ties that keep democracy strong at the local level, whatever it is we need to strengthen the ties that bind us all. In order to keep democracy strong, we've absolutely got to do that at the local level. We've got to have these little cells of democracy and make those cells as big as we can because they'll take them longer to find us lock us up." If you remember our discussion of Foucault at the beginning of the book, this is exactly what he means: if we make power diffuse, they can't catch all of us.

Find Your People, Even in Hostile Places

I am a bit hopeful because I think we couldn't possibly have lost everything that our predecessors built here.

—A VOTING RIGHTS ACTIVIST FROM WISCONSIN, 2018

It's easy to feel isolated doing this work, particularly when circumstance or geography make you feel alone. However, you can find people anywhere—or use the internet to create your own network.

One thing that I've changed my mind about over the years—I think much of America is more purple than our topline numbers give us credit for. We also have an end-of-history mentality about red states that keeps us from thinking of them as competitive. Even so, there are continual talks about redrawing the map. (Spend some time googling—there are some great suggestions out there. Merge the Dakotas into a MegaKota! Chop off part of Oregon and give it to Idaho! Texas should be its own country! Split California into three states!) I had this section entitled "Lessons from Red America," but I realized instead that many places in "blue" America can be hostile as well. For example, Lincoln and Omaha have very active Democratic parties, often win closely contested elections, and are well organized—they are a formidable blue force in a very red state. On the other hand, my area of Brooklyn is very conservative in a lot of ways.[9] Even democratic candidates talk about school safety and fiscal responsibility and other coded terms, there is almost no democratic ground game, and you don't see a lot of progressive organizing.

Learning from what worked

Progressive organizers were able to establish themselves in inhospitable parts of the country, building resistance in hostile places. I learned important history lessons through these conversations with organizers about what their states were like *before* becoming ruby-red. Fighting in every state, in every locale, matters—particularly because people in every community deserve basic human rights, health care, and reproductive freedom. The 2016 election, paradoxically, made people less convinced that the red/state blue state divide was impenetrable; it forced people to find solutions.

1. You have more allies than you think. In states that voted red in 2016, many activists were propelled into action for the first time; a Texan shared this reflection: "I'm in a very red county in a very red state, and people are willing to stand up and say 'hey, something's not right about this' and I am willing to put my body on the line and raise my voice." As liberals emerged from the election downtrodden and looking for community, they were shocked to find "like-minded people" in their communities they'd never encountered before. One Democrat from rural Texas shared ruefully, "I have always felt like a very rare bird." This changed after the election: there was a powerful shift from a sense that being progressive was a solitary identity to the beginning of a *collective* identity. If you've ever been the only nursing mom in an office of men, or the only openly gay kid in school, or the only atheist at Thanksgiving dinner with your evangelical cousins, you know the power of one becoming many: of other parents advocating for family-friendly policies, of other kids coming out and realizing that you're in good company, of your uncle confiding that he hasn't been to church in 30 years either. This is of course the abiding power of the #MeToo movement. This was the ironic truth of the election: the backlash was so public and so fierce that people realized they were not the only Clinton voters in their towns. Activists in deep-red areas of the country found ways to seek each other out. Georgie, a protester you met earlier in the book, was chatting to a woman at a party who whispered, "I'm a community organizer." Georgie looked around, bent over, and whispered back, "We need to talk." From that moment, she had a new ally.

2. All elections can be winnable. In 2017, Doug Jones, a Democrat, ran for Senate in Alabama (yes, the state that went for Trump by almost 30 points in 2016—that Alabama). Doug Jones, once thought a longshot, was pushed into the lead in the race when Roy Moore, his opponent, was accused weeks before the election of sexually assaulting teenage girls.

The idea that Doug Jones had a real chance breathed life into the campaign. As one progressive organizer from the state told me: "Everybody who had a more moderate—let alone liberal—point of view just kept their mouth shut and their head down. And with Trump and then Roy Moore, it was just like 'Well, fuck this shit . . . no! Not just no, but hell no! Enough! This is something we must change!' So we did."

At first, working on the Jones campaign felt futile. Over time, though, they realized that there was more hidden support for the progressive candidate than the popular media narrative was leading people to believe: "But the more we knocked on doors, the more we realized that the conventional wisdom came from the fact that all the people like us had been keeping their mouths shut." By no longer keeping their mouths shut, they started a cascade effect of that normalized voting for Democrats. And, Doug Jones won (at least that time)— Alabama sent a Democrat to the Senate in 2017. If Alabama can do it, so can your state.

Embrace Different Time Horizons

This is not the old age I had envisioned for myself; I thought it would be very peaceful. But I'll continue to do my hobbling old lady bit.

—AN OCTOGENARIAN ACTIVIST FROM CALIFORNIA, 2018

How do you sustain local activism? If everything feels critical, you might get a swell of support, but then people fade away during maintenance phases. With too much of a lead up, however, people drift before you get to the part where the movement is sustainable. The trick is to alternate between time horizons, long and short, actions, direct and systemic.

This is critically important: it makes sure you're not a rapid response squad that jumps from issue to issue, which leads to burnout and a failure to consider things systemically. Slow organizing sustains community building.

DISPATCHES FROM THE FIELD 16:
CONFLICT OVER FAMILIES BELONG TOGETHER

The debate over the Families Belong Together rallies in June 2018 underscores the complexity of negotiations between groups with different visions. It's easy to see why. The family separation policy was brutal—separating children from their families at the border, causing unimaginable psychological damage along with the physical and sexual abuse the kids were subjected to.

When news started to break about the children being held in cages at the border, I was sick to my stomach, not sleeping for days. I was crisscrossing the country at the time, attending protests from Texas to Idaho Falls, watching how red states dealt with the crisis.

On the surface, Families Belong Together was an enormous, unmitigated success for the Resistance. However, underneath revealed a fundamental chasm between local and national organizers. Local immigration groups wanted to not just focus on families, but instead a broad panoply of issues that had led to this point. Moveon.org, who pushed out the nationwide rallies in coordination with Indivisible, insisted on the focus on families, not immigration issues more broadly.

Elena, a national-level organizer deeply involved in immigrant rights work, mused to me that it was a tough moment—on the one hand, it was very much the local immigration groups' time to shine: "MoveOn sent out a call, and we signed up to lead that rally. Many, many immigrant groups in the town, many undocumented who have family in Mexico. So, we partnered with them to come up with a program that would tell those stories and get people energized, and we raised about $10,000 to donate to those border groups to get legal help for the asylum seekers. I mean, it's hard. Can't split the babies from their mommies. You just cannot do that."

On the other hand, the national groups were there with the coordination, ready to orchestrate a media spectacle. One activist articulated a double bind: the organizers who had been doing this front-line work for years below the radar and not getting much attention, and then the political professionals stepped in. As one organizer told me: "My attitude is always we're allies with them, we really respect what they've done in the past and what they do is important, but we shouldn't be afraid to take a different approach or to try something new . . . it's time for innovation, and we respect their opinion, and we want to help them succeed, but we're not going to let them tell us that what we're doing is not what needs to be done, and that we just need to send volunteers to go door knock." Hartford, Connecticut, canceled its rally because of irreconcilable differences between the groups.

The conflicts were broader than the rally—in one instance, a local Indivisible group wanted to shut down an ICE building, but local immigrant groups said needed immigration services were located there. As Elena put it: "Are we trusting the actual people who deal with the organization about whether it's right to shut the whole building down? Sometimes you're going to be right and sometimes you're going to be wrong . . . but at least people are having control of their own lives, rather than being pushed around all the time."

The Hartford rally was canceled in deference to a coalition of immigrant rights groups, although angry organizers referred to the cancelation as shooting themselves in the foot: "We had an issue with the immigrant rights groups here, not feeling that that day of action a few weeks ago was appropriate. A big meeting, a big rally in Hartford was canceled because of the immigrants' rights groups not feeling that the messaging that was put out by MoveOn was correct. And you're like 'oh my God, why don't we just shoot ourselves?' It's just awful." A Connecticut activist explained to me that the immigrant groups in the community wanted an anti-ICE rally, not a family-centered rally. Her group told them: "Look, we'll promote the ICE action. We will ask families to go. We will do everything we can to steer people at the rally to the next day." But in the end, it wasn't enough.

Elena also reflected on the meaning of the internal clashes on the left over the Families Belong Together rallies. As she told me, "There's a lot of really, really meaningful, really good organizing happening in local communities, and those activists get really upset when national organizations amplify it without giving proper credit, and that's real, that's absolutely real. When we do this work, we need to be thoughtful about giving proper credit and putting the people that are leading the work on the front stage . . . we need to be better partners about making sure that folks that aren't big are also seen."

Learning from what worked

The need for different time horizons was echoed by community builders who felt constrained by the rapid response feeling of Indivisible. As one organizer said:

> When you're focusing across the board on quick wins and quick action, you don't get to go deep into any issues. So, then when you interact with groups who are like immigrant rights groups, or gay rights groups, or gun violence groups, or police brutality groups, or whatever, it ends up being a really superficial interaction, because you end up saying like "this week we're interested in Dreamers, next week we're interested in mass incarceration, the week after, we're suddenly interested in detention centers."

Tanisha's analysis of what communities need makes this clear. "We know that Trump needs to be dismantled real quick, but how do we dismantle, maybe from the inside—a system that works the way it's supposed to work? It's not broken—the way it's working intentionally doesn't work for Black and Brown folks. So we ask politicians: when we vote you in, how will you undo this?" How can you be nimble enough to move between strategically endorsing some politicians, but then maintain enough of a degree of separation that you continue to put pressure on them once the election cycle is over?

But also . . .

Even as we build a community that reflects the progressive world we want for our friends and children, we can't ignore the violence and mental health issues are endemic in activist communities. We need to talk about violence within and against activists, and make part of our organizing the creation of spaces that are safe for all people. Here's what I learned from listening to activists talk. Violence can come from the outside, and can also come from within activist spaces.

We need to:

- be aware of, and subvert, violence
- create mentally well spaces
- recognize burnout.

Be Aware of, and Subvert, Violence

For 90 percent of the research for this book, I took my kids to protests across the country. And then, I stopped—partially because of COVID, and then because of the laws that allow protesters to be run over with cars. This became psychological, always lurking in my brain as a possibility—and it has grown larger over time. My son had a field trip in lower Manhattan the day that Trump was arraigned on one set of charges or another (who can keep track, really?), and I wrote an email asking his teacher to keep him off the sidewalks—because I didn't know what Trump supporters might do. Even though everything was fine, the psychic risk of protesting feels different to me now than it did five years ago.

After the fourth (or fifteenth or seventy-second) mass shooting happened, I told my husband, "No sane person raises their kids in this culture." I started the laborious process of claiming my Irish citizenship . . . just in case. "Are you running away?" my dad asked me. "I'm not sacrificing my kids to the gun nuts and fascists," I snapped. We're still here . . . but the soft hypocrisy of this book is that I don't know how long we'll stay.

Learning from the past

Certain activist communities I talked to were constantly under stress because of violence—something I didn't expect at first. Of course, there was Charlottesville, and the death of the Heather Heyer there, and the Ferguson leaders who continue to turn up dead. [📢] The attempted kidnapping of Michigan governor Gretchen Whitmer further drove home the danger of the moment; as one activist told me, that moment underscored to her the stakes of the danger. [🔊] "I think we've shown the underbelly of America that many liberals like me thought had disappeared. I never really understood Timothy McVeigh but that's all I could think about when I saw what they were trying to do to Governor Whitmer." [🔊] The threat of violence was pervasive in an increasing number of local protests as well: "We have these clusters of machine gun–toting rednecks that are walking around the city and going to marches. How dare they? They've taken over the parks. They walk around drinking with a fucking machine gun on their shoulder and the cops do nothing," an activist from the Northeast told me in 2020.

The violence, or threats of violence, came from the state as well. One health care activist, whose husband had been arrested, talked with me about the utter inhumanity of arresting health care activists and disabled protesters: "We get people arrested every week because every week we have a fight in Congress."

Local police also engaged in bullying tactics against activists. Memphis, the only majority Black city in Tennessee, had a history of bullying protesters: the ACLU sued Memphis's police department for violating a consent decree from the 1970s, which prohibited spying on organizers. A local activist described how police would follow around protesters even when they were just eating lunch, as well as show up to intimidate participants at protests. As one organizer told me, "Massive drones fly over every demonstration except when ladies march . . . they stay home then."

Of course, community members also perpetrated violence, harassment, and intimidation. An activist from the South received hostile Facebook messages from a Trump supporter describing where everyone in their Indivisible group sat during organizing meetings: a clear sign of surveillance and intimidation. Another activist told me about the high stakes of protesting in Florida: "I'm always looking over my shoulder. It's more dangerous in Florida. Florida is the NRA's proving ground, the NRA's stomping ground. You just assume everybody in Florida who's ticked off has a gun . . ."

Activists I spoke with were also threatened by the militia for the Aryan Nation and the American Redoubt in the Northwest; [📢] one told me "they're just convinced that the government's gonna fall and they're gonna be here to pick up the pieces and they're moving into our area and just trying to fucking ruin my town. We hate them." Of course, the January 6 insurrection was the ultimate proof that these groups were organized and willing to use violent means to overturn the result of democratic elections. As one person remarked, talking to me in 2017 felt safer in many ways than talking to me in 2020.

Recognize Burnout

Activism is an activity with a high level of burnout, in part due to community violence, but also because of all of the high stakes nature of organizing. People suffer real trauma, mentally and sometimes physically, because of their work, a sacrifice we should value as the beneficiaries of their labor. A slow approach to organizing can help with this: recognizing that you can bow out sometimes, and that the work will still go on and welcome you when you can participate again.

Some activists attribute their burnout to the emotional damage they attributed to Biden's predecessor, and others to the nature of organizing itself. As one person told me, "The truth is, everyone that's doing this work is really fucking tired. We are throwing all of our ideas at the wall and seeing what sticks."[10] The stress from the Trump administration was, at times, toxic, and even the people most engaged in pushing back against the administration at times felt confused and angry about having to be constantly on alert. As one person put it, "I didn't want this—I didn't ask to do this;" activists wanted their lives back and a break from the constant pressure to save their communities.[11] Organizing, for them, wasn't their "normal." They hoped the

Resistance would be like a surgical strike that would excise the cancer and let the healthy, though imperfect, body politic get on with its life.[12]

Activists described themselves as permanently destabilized— caught in cycles of anxiety and uncertainty. The long-term, cumulative impact of organizing on mental health is something that is only peripherally acknowledged in the activist community, despite the pervasive history of depression and suicide[13] in the community. Georgie, who you met in Dispatch 4, shared this with me: "After my first season lobbying, my idealism got so smashed, I went into depression and had to go on anti-depressants, my first time because I was so distraught over what I saw." One organizer had a friend doing immigration work who "organized herself literally into the hospital . . . the mental toll of taking on that much trauma and support of other people all on her own was too much."

On the other hand, activism also was a respite for a number of the activists I spoke to, providing a safe haven from threats to their mental health: "I think the number one thing protesting has done is convince me and others that we are not alone, screaming into the void." For some people, activism offered a way out of the sense of existential dread: "Action helps a lot; it's better to do something than nothing because that's when the angst moves in. Just keep doing." Building community, feeling like you are fighting and organizing for what's right, can have a real impact on staving off depression.

The Remedy: Stay Soft, Create Safe Spaces

Push into the world what you wish to create. If I can work hard at staying soft enough to hear the people around me and gather with others to move a progressive agenda forward, it will help me survive.

—A REPRODUCTIVE RIGHTS ACTIVIST FROM TEXAS

DISPATCHES FROM THE FIELD 17:
THE RESISTANCE TAKES A BREATHER

When I talked to people after the 2018 midterms, they were taking a deep breath. Figuring out where to commit their energy. Many were intensely angry—angry about the Kavanaugh nomination, angry about the Senate, angry about the family separation policy. When I asked one person what was next for him, he sounded conflicted. He told me that he hadn't been an activist before 2016, and he had only gotten involved because of what he felt was an existential threat to his democracy. Now that 2018 had happened, that the wave had succeeded, it was time to take a deep breath and refocus. He was taking music lessons, hanging out with the democratic socialists, and trying to figure out what was next. Another activist who volunteered for Beto O'Rourke's campaign told me she was done. She was planning to commit herself to a needle exchange program in her town, become a phlebotomist. Others called after the election to tell me their Indivisible chapter had dissolved, or that they had resigned from their boards.

Of course, the exhaustion of organizing led people to want to take a break from politics. As one person reminded me: "A lot of people in the Indivisible movement are new to political activism. Now that we'll have a more normal presidency, they feel like they can maybe take a break. I know that activists across the country are exhausted, just completely exhausted. I could see folks needing time to sit back. But we certainly are going to continue our work." The end of the Trump administration was protracted and painful. Many of the protesters I talked to on the left were exhausted and bitter, and felt denied the sweetness of the victory they'd worked so hard for. It could be, in part, the four excruciating days between when polls closed on November 3, 2020, and when the race was finally called on November 7, 2020. It could be that both Georgia Senate races—which held the keys to control of the Senate—were decided on January 6, 2021, as the insurrection was taking place. It could be that the people most deserving of taking a victory lap were bruised, bloodied (often literally), and so disgusted with the system that they were left worrying about the next step of democracy instead of celebrating its salvation.

As we limped over the 2020 finish line—with the photo-finish Senate races in Georgia deciding the fate of the Senate, and the country, and with the insurrection of January 6 telegraphing the right's unwillingness to accept the outcome of the election, the mood among activists I talked to was curious. No one was talking about organizing against January 6, or what that meant for the future of democracy. Most of them were going back to their day jobs, though those day jobs had shifted over time. Many of them had run for office themselves, taken jobs on congressional staffs and local campaigns, become political commentators, and made documentaries. Only a few were talking to me about how to sustain the momentum of the campaign.

Rather than being relieved, they were angry and exhausted. One activist I talked to frequently over the course of the project advised me: "You have a PhD. You should be able to leave the country. Get your kids the hell out of here." Even after wresting the country back from the brink, activists still couldn't imagine the country turning the direction they want it to go. Another one told me: "I'll be an activist until I die, just because it's in my bones, it's just who I am . . . right now, it's just really depressing."

Sure enough, the activists started telling me this. As one put it succinctly: "We don't want to resist forever." Another told me that people in her group were envisioning a return to the "no drama Obama" days. As one career activist told me, "Not everybody in that group is an old activist like me. They were people who took time out of their life to make a change . . . because they felt it was necessary. I think they want to go back to some kind of new normal, whatever that is." Trump's defeat was in many ways a surrendering of the guard, a turning over of the key to protecting the kingdom to the Democrats.

Non-Indivisible people were more likely to tell me that the protests would continue regardless of who was elected (perhaps over-estimating the appetite of people to keep it up, or underestimating their willingness to go home). In one of our talks, Tanisha started laughing: "I hate to tell you, mediocre men kill me." You could hear her rolling her eyes over the telephone. "I'm like 'oh my God the patriarchy.' Our vow had been, we don't give a shit who gets voted in, we're still going to be on the streets. We'll be in the streets until we get change. Because here's the deal, there's millions of people in the streets right now for change. That's what an uprising's supposed to do. If you're a really great leader, you say, we need to listen to the people. Because we vote, you win. The people have a right to challenge you . . . I'm hoping." This insistence on hoping that this is not just a moment stuck with me. I hope that in the spirit of this book, it sticks with you too.

What do we do? How can we both embed our work in our communities and also protect ourselves when communities become toxic or violent? Part of the answer is that being involved with this kind of work requires a balance of emotions—staying angry enough to be engaged, but also angry about the fact you have to be engaged—and using that as a way to set the boundaries to stay soft.[14] If that feels like an impossible contradiction, it is. As one activist said: "You've got to do self-care. You've got to say no, you've got to step back. You ain't going to fix it all. You can't go to every meeting." You need to create spaces that aren't only demanding your energy, but also giving you what you need to put that energy back into the world and your work.

Learning from the past

1. Pay attention to productive anger. The idea of productive anger—of rage—comes up in Brittany Cooper's *Eloquent Rage,* in Rebecca Traister's *Good and Mad,* and in interviews with activists. When the world is on fire, we need to be mad, and to stay mad. As one organizer said: "It's been clear for a long time that collective rage has been building, and activists want to tamp that down instead of guide it in a constructive direction. It doesn't work. This rage is legitimate and justified. Activists who disagree miss the mark." To channel and use this anger, we need community.

2. Seek communion. One organizer used the metaphor of a church to describe what would be needed in order to heal trauma in communities:

> Individual trauma is unwieldy. Collective trauma is near impossible to manage, control, guide, and heal. John Lewis has always guided my view of civil rights work. To me, the concept of church is vital. Whether it's a literal faith community or a small community that provides intimate support, recuperation, and shelter from the storm, those little houses are imperative to progress. To me, that's

what's missing in the mass social movements. There are too many undifferentiated experiences coalescing at a high volume. To me, without a church, without an ability to care for the people that the cause is meant to represent, that's not civil rights.

Another way to think about this idea of church is through the creation of safe spaces, community forms of care are one way to help members of the community survive through burnout and illness. Two of the Black activists I talked to had shifted their focus to providing mental health care for their community. As Rosa said: "At the moment right now where I am, it's creating safe spaces. Recognizing that safe spaces look different and understanding that the very rigid structure that we have set up for ourselves is not realistic for times like this. This is a crisis and people need to be able to handle this crisis as what's best for them and not meet expectations that are not realistic for them." Processing that trauma is critical to doing the work of building a safe community.

3. Avoid navel gazing. Other long-term activists spoke derisively about the "newly woke" coming to movements looking to validate their feelings without actually doing the hard work of organizing—what one called the "world is hard let's drink tea" version of pseudo-activism. This tension, which also had serious class underpinnings, felt like a real sticking point among the old vanguard of activists, one of whom referred to this particular brand of organizing as a return to the human potential movement of the 1980s. She said:

> But what's really struck me is all of this self-care stuff that keeps popping up [activists] on social media with messages like 'go walk on a beach for a while,' and the response is 'bitch, I work three jobs. You want me to go take a walk on the beach? Do you know how much of America doesn't have time to go walk on the beach? Do you know how privileged that is?' They are calling the self-care civil rights

work, but they're not talking about community organizing, this is 'better living through feeling your feelings.[15]

bell hooks (2020) has something to say on this point as well: "I am often struck by the dangerous narcissism fostered by spiritual rhetoric that pays so much attention to individual self-improvement and so little to the practice of love within the context of community." If you build community, you are doing the work that it takes to support yourself *and* the other people in your space. It is generative, instead of inwardly focused. Part of this is acknowledging that resistance is exhausting—I heard "we don't want to resist forever" more times than I could count. But instead of stopping, work on a new future by moving from a space of resistance to a space of normalizing activism: constantly working to create the world you want to live in.

4. Move toward sustainability. Community wellness is key to individual wellness. As one organizer said, "we need to push for more flexibility for people to be able to give to their communities. It's good for mental health, it's good for our well-being, it's good for our communities, and it's good for our children. **We shouldn't have to be so busy trying to survive our culture that we can't give back to our culture."**

In Sum: Protect Your Community and Your People

Again, this chapter focused on the three core elements of organizing according to our CSI principles:

Constant—When you look at your community as the place for your activism, instead of the country, you realize it *has* to be constant. We should always be finding some way or another to make our communities better.

Slow—Communities, like families, have norms, values, histories embedded in them. As in the Scotland and Ireland examples in the intro, this kind of consensus requires deep work. Conversation, consensus building, real attempts to understand how other people envision their future in the community.

Inclusive—To keep your communities safe, you need to build spaces where everyone can be well—where people inside of your community and out can thrive.

This chapter is full of contradictions and tensions. How do you protect yourself and also not quit? How do you build community and also push back against communal violence? How do you reconcile the system you're railing against with the desire to recruit and register voters in deep-red parts of the country? The system has always been terrible and it's terrible not because it's broken but because it's working as designed (as Michelle Alexander and so many others remind us)—that is the part of this. Because I wondered, even as I talked to all these truly amazing people who had put their lives on hold, gotten arrested, been driven out of their communities, been harassed by cops—I wondered if the system would ever *let* actual change happen.

As Kat, the Texas harm reduction community organizer, reflected:

> America has always been this way, and I think that's kind of sad, you know. It's a bummer to think about me being eight years old, and stoked for the Fourth of July, because of the fireworks, and wearing a flag proudly. Now seeing myself, I'm ashamed of my race, ashamed of my country, and ashamed of a lot of things I was proud of back then, because I was so young. It's just a weird time. It's different than the other times.

We hung up shortly after, and that conversation stuck with me. I was also that little girl. I remember taking part in Taekwondo performances as a nine-year-old, singing "I'm Proud to be an American" as the promise of the end of the Cold War loomed. (The words *at least* do a lot of work in that song, don't they?) [📢] I wonder if my parents felt any irony at those moments, or if they were just proud of me for getting on stage and being happy to participate in performative nationalism.

I constantly wonder if the way we're raising our kids is the right way. My son watched *Colin in Black and White* on Netflix and then stopped saying the pledge of allegiance. ("Sometimes I mouth it so I don't get in trouble," he tells me.) Our friend from Florida came to visit, and my son greeted him with "Ron DeSantis, what an asshole, am I right?" Is this the best way to raise a politically motivated kiddo? How can I also make sure he knows that Gretchen Whitmer is an amazing governor? It's all hard. BUT—it's a reason why we need to get better at telling our own stories, and then retelling the stories of others.

DEMOCRACY: A FIGHT SONG (AND A LOVE LETTER TO EVERYONE SAVING IT)

DISPATCHES FROM THE FIELD 18:
THE WAR ON DEMOCRACY CONTINUES

I've tried to keep these dispatches short, but this last one is important: a warning about how conservative actors are trying to ban *political participation* from being taught in schools. This whole book has been about how democracy is something you *do,* a set of skills we enact together. In John Dewey's "Democracy and Education," he writes: "A democracy is more than a form of government; it is primarily a mode of associated living, of conjoint communicated experience."

And so, conservatives are trying to ban that.

Around the country, democratic participation is under attack. Texas, unsurprisingly, has taken this the furthest, deciding to sever the relationship between students and government; the legislation was authored by conservative commentator Stanley Kurtz and championed by conservative organizations such as the National Academy of Scholars (NAS) and Civics Alliance. It was signed into law as part of a broader bill without much fanfare in 2021, and was relatively unnoticed until The Guardian broke news of it in 2023. Although places like Hillsdale College have garnered national attention for their 1776 Curriculum and nationwide network of charter schools, what distinguishes the efforts of NAS and Civic Alliance is their blatant emphasis on removing skills and active learning from the curriculum.

Texas is the only state so far to affirmatively ban assignments that have students participate in the political process (though South Carolina introduced the same bill in 2021). However, this is part of a broader movement to change not just what *content* is taught in schools (manifested through the so-called CRT debate) but, more alarmingly, banning schools from teaching students that democracy is *participatory*.

In 2022, right-wing political action committees like the 1776 Project endorsed far-right candidates in school board races across the country, including in the small town of Woodland Park, Colorado, which became the first place in the country to adopt the American Birthright social studies standards written by NAS.

American Birthright overtly opposes civic engagement, arguing that it is "substitute vocational training in progressive activism." Indeed, as Kathryn Joyce noted in Salon last year, the document is by design *not* a curriculum, but instead provides a "model set of social studies standards, of the sort that state-level education departments adopt in order to guide and regulate individual school districts as they craft their own curricula." It is a political guide masquerading as a curriculum. David Randall, NAS's research director, is somewhat incredibly quoted as saying: "It is terribly important to be a disengaged citizen, and indeed, a disengaged student."

In some states, conservative advocacy to remove skills from civics standards has worked. South Dakota, after consulting with Hillsdale College, rewrote its social studies standards this year. In the far-right magazine the *Daily Signal*, Ben Jones, South Dakota's state historian, called the new standards a model for putting "content and knowledge at the center of things" because they "excavate the John Dewey progressive notion about skills."

Meanwhile, Florida's new standards, which "promote American exceptionalism and focus more on foundational concepts, while downplaying simulations, student projects, and other participatory approaches," flattens a three-dimensional vision of citizenship into rote lessons. Students used to be asked to register to vote or to communicate with government officials. That standard has been replaced with the requirement to analyze the influences of ancient Greece, Rome, and the Judeo-Christian tradition. Holding a mock election has been replaced with studying the nation's founding documents. Conducting a service project has been replaced with understanding the advantages of capitalism. These curricular revisions aren't just academic: they fundamentally reorient the relationship between students and their government.

This isn't just bad for democracy—it's bad teaching.

Even in states that haven't officially adopted this curriculum, it's become a kind of conservative calling card. In North Carolina, a state representative tried (and failed) to pass a law authorizing Beaufort County Public Schools to teach the Hillsdale curriculum instead of the state standards. There were echoes of this on the 2022 campaign trail as well. Kari Lake, the conservative nominee for governor of Arizona, endorsed the Hillsdale curriculum; Ryan Walters, who was elected as Oklahoma's Secretary of Education in 2022, campaigned on having every teacher in Oklahoma undergo training by Hillsdale.

Because John Dewey envisioned democracy as a living thing, he believed that it wouldn't persist in perpetuity, but rather needed to be reborn each generation; for him, education was the "midwife" of democracy. Champions of public education throughout our country's history have believed that schools are, above all else, places where we create a vision for the kinds of citizens we want to be in charge of the next generation. If not, we risk students tuning out of lessons—and missing the part where they learn to change the world.

Writing a book takes a long time, and I was often worried that this book might "miss its moment," that politics as usual might seem boring and old hat by the time this book was ready to see light of day.

This was a common fear in the waning days of the Trump presidency; a real sense that people would go back to a business-as-usual, "leave politics to the politicians" approach to things. There was no need to worry because we aren't, to quote Jon Favreau (the podcasting guy), sufficiently out of the wilderness. We have spent the Biden administration figuring out how to save democracy against a future where Republicans seize power (and then refuse to let go) or infighting about the conflicts on the Democratic side of the aisle. What we haven't done is adequately assess our victories. Because the war isn't won, we haven't celebrated the battle—which means we won't know what to do next time we need to mobilize again. As I hope this book has persuaded you, bell hooks is right about the need to constantly center politics, no matter what the critics say. This passage from the lovely *Dancing with Words* is worth reading in full:

> To engage a politics of transformation we surrender the need to occupy a space of hedonistic intellectual "cool" that overtly embraces old notions of objectivity and neutrality. Certainly, I and my work are often seen as not cool enough precisely because there is always an insistence on framing ideas politically and calling for active resistance.

Let's join hooks at the table for uncool kids, and insist on eschewing neutrality for a politics of resistance.

The World Will Always Need Saving

It's hard to adapt to the idea that we live in a world that may always be a little bit on fire; that we may never return to a place where it's possible to tune out politics for a while to focus on creating a sustainable community where we can breathe. We know that Mr. Rogers tells us that, when times are scary, we should look for the helpers, and I think that's true. I hope this book encourages you to become a helper, to find the moments of engagement that are important and to reach out.

I also think it's important to look for the organizers and the activists—particularly those who are brave enough to take stances against popular opinion. I mentioned earlier the bravery of the protesters turning out week after week in Israel in 2023 against Netanyahu and for democracy, who ultimately were able to get the government to blink and roll back some of their court reforms. In October 2023, hundreds of Jewish Americans were arrested at the US Capitol for protesting *in favor* of the rights of Gazans. Although politics is complicated and life is long, people are, almost always, better than their governments. And since then, we've seen massive anti-genocide marches around the country. And when the world is on fire, look for those people. Their bravery will break your heart.

Normalizing the Struggle

All of us need to learn that is resistance as a way of life, one that permeates our decisions, becomes part of our fabric. Not resist and done, not protest and then let politicians deal with it. We don't need to be on all the time—indeed we can't be—but we always need to be thinking about, on the backburner, how we're making our democracy, our civic, public, shared life better.

Constant—when you discover your "why," and manifest an activist identity, it's not something to turn off. You are learning how to shift into a constant, slow-burning, mode of resistance. By saying "I will" instead of "you should," you're orienting yourself toward action.

Slow—it isn't jumping from one thing to the next, but figuring out where you fit, listening to stories, getting the lay of the land in your town.

Inclusive—You are using a universal design framework to make sure that everyone can find a seat at your table and you're taking leadership from people who don't look like you.

The thing about this model is that it works for everyone. You don't need to vow never to drive again, never to use Amazon again, to never see your racist uncle again (it's complicated, I get it) to still be working toward a society that is more just and inclusive. You just need to be committed to being in the struggle. If you remember the greengrocer and T Swift, the act of not hanging a sign or rerecording a catalog is worth more than all of the protests you could stage.

Let's take the example of the prisoner's dilemma. In game theory,[1] the prisoner's dilemma occurs when two actors (individuals, states, etc.) have two choices: cooperate or defect. Fortunately for us, there was a British show that illustrated the concept of the prisoner's dilemma perfectly, it was called . . . wait for it . . . "Golden Balls." In the final round of the game, the two remaining contestants have two choices: to split the jackpot or to steal the jackpot. If both choose split, they share it 50–50. If both choose steal, neither gets any money. But, if one chooses split and the other steals, then the dastardly stealer gets the whole jackpot—leaving the trusting splitter with nothing.

Think about it:

- If you both defect, then neither of you win, but neither of you lose. Second-worst outcome.
- If you defect and they cooperate, you win, and they are a sucker. Best outcome!
- If you cooperate and they defect, then you are a sucker, and they win. WORST OUTCOME OF ALL.
- If you both cooperate, then you both win—but by no means guaranteed. Second best outcome.

What should you do? If you're just going to have that one interaction, you should probably defect. But everything changes if you're going to have more than one interaction. If, in fact, you're going to see each other more because you're bound together (by community, social norms, treaties, working together, or any of the other myriad reasons humans are constantly cooperative) then cooperation becomes your best option. When we have relationships with and responsibilities toward other people, it makes sense to cooperate. If someone defects, they are sanctioned for it and the social norm of cooperation is reinforced. Indeed, as organizers Kelly Hayes and Mariame Kaba wrote in 2023 in the *Boston Review*, saving the world almost inevitably requires some solidarity with people who are not like you: "To create movements, rather than clubhouses, we need to engage with people with whom we do not fully identify and may even dislike." You don't have to be best friends, but you do have to keep coming back to the table.

Four Steps Is All It Takes

When the world feels overwhelming, it can be helpful to ask—what step am I at right now? Where is my place? What am I working toward? These steps aren't linear, necessarily: you can always go back as your time and attention shift. For example, I have a clear vision of what I think a democratic future for the country should look like, and education is a cornerstone of this (Step One: Envision a Democratic Future). I've been increasingly upset about the move to ban books from schools. I think it's one of the most dangerous things we can do in a democracy. At first, I struggled to figure out what I could do besides getting angry and following stories about book banning (Step Two: Find Your Why). Then, when word leaked that Scholastic was creating a diversity catalog that schools/districts needed to opt into, I had an "in." I started talking with my kids' school about our policy on these things. I found other parents who agreed with me (Step Three: Find Your People). I wrote letters and shared them in my circles in case other parents wanted to put pressure on their own schools. I signed up to speak at the school board meeting (Step Four: Mobilizing). I also started following PEN America and all of the awesome librarians on social media and writing more about the topic, trying to make this not just an issue of the day, but something that can sustain my time and focus. These four steps can help you figure out how you want to intervene. Luckily, Scholastic backed down, because thousands of people used this formula to put pressure on them.

Can We Save the World?

One question that every reader who has gotten to this point should ask: did protest work? If I'm asking you to adopt an adversarial mindset, and never let go of it, you deserve to think about whether doing so will actually have an impact. Indeed, from Vincent Bevins's recent *If We Burn* to Fredrik DeBoer's *How Elites Ate the Social Justice Movement* to wondering how the heck we wound up living in a world where progressives "won" but states are pulling books with gay kids off shelves to throwing moms in jail for getting their daughter abortion pills, it's easy to feel like we've lost.

And yet . . . it seems to me like there's a real case to be made that all of the phone calls and meetings and marches and fundraisers and basement roundtables and book clubs convinced people that democracy was worth fighting for. That we were given a glimpse of the better angels of our nature, and allowed to keep it for a little while longer. And maybe we haven't disbanded or decommissioned, maybe we didn't run out of steam but maybe we're just resting, gearing up for the next battle.

Another way to view things is that American protest is, and always has been, ruthlessly pragmatic. Would major protests against *Dobbs* have overturned the law? No, but these anti-choice politicians sure are being punished at the ballot box.[2] Where can we make a change? How can we get skin back in the game? That's the decision you're going to have to make in the months and years to follow.

And I won't pretend that I think it's easy. I won't pretend that I'm always engaged or do much more besides vote and complain and write.

But I believe that when people think the world needs to change, it can and will. As I said in the introduction, saving our democracy isn't easy, but it's far simpler than we think. If we stay constantly engaged, and we create a legacy of activism, then we will win. Indeed, the Varieties of Democracy report I told you about in the intro? The one that warned us about losing our democracy? The 2023 theme is "Defiance in the Face of Autocratization" (Papada et al., 2023). In the report, they cite cases of democracies bouncing back from the brink of autocracy. The most common theme? "Large-scale popular mobilization against the incumbent." We've mounted one of these once, and we can do it again. It's not all good news—for the first time in 20 years there are more closed societies than liberal democracies—but there's real evidence that protest works against anti-democratic forces.

Over the course of this book, I wanted to create a three-way dialogue: between you, the reader, and the future of the movement; the activists who gave me their time and insight so we could learn what worked and not repeat the mistakes of the past; and the scholars and thinkers and writers who have spent their life studying what makes protest work across the world. But to be clear, that doesn't work without you breathing life and ideas into our democracy. Taking the movement and making it your own. As I hope you felt throughout the book, I felt a deep sense of kinship with many of the activists I interviewed over time. I thought about them, rooted for them, was excited to catch up. And as crazy as it sounds, I feel that same sense of kinship with you. I can't wait to see what you do next with this book. After all, Justice Sotomayor told us that the meaning of the Constitution is found "in the spirit of the people who live under it." And that spirit is feisty.

The After Party:

A (VERY) BRIEF HISTORY OF ACTIVISM IN THE US

This book isn't a history of activism in the United States, and I'm not a historian. However, the book covers a lot of ground, both topically and chronologically. To help navigate that terrain, this is my very brief, incomplete guide to organizing in the United States (and a little bit in Europe). If history's your thing—enjoy! If not, then I'd bookmark this chapter and come back to it as you need to when you encounter a reference that you're not completely sure about.[1]

I also wrote this chapter because it's so easy to forget how *eventful* things were. Even just skimming through the next 4,500 words will likely trigger memories of some event you've forgotten. Obviously, there are huge swaths of the American resistance story that aren't told here—like the generations of struggle against enslavement, for example, or the injustices against Korematsu and millions of Japanese Americans during WWII. There's no mention of environmental movements, and virtually nothing on antifa or the DSA or Indigenous movements or the WTO protests in Seattle in the late 1990s. Those all belong in a rounded history of activism in the United States, and this is not one.

I only discuss events that come up in the book, both so this chapter can act as a kind of reference, and because these are the stories that are foundational in the lives of the activists profiled in these chapters. If you are frustrated that your favorite activist event is left out, you should tell that story. I'll listen.

Early Times through 1900

I won't pretend to do justice to a history of the resistance and oppression that began at our founding as colonies, but I will suggest the 1619 Project as a way to immerse yourself in the racialized history of the United States.

The United States as a country was born from activism. The decision to break away from our oppressors (sorry England) and to declare our independence was nothing short of a monumental feat of organizing (one person told me that her family's history of activism dated back to when they would hide ammunition from the Brits during the war). We've been a rebellious people from the start. Of course, no doubt, power relations form and reform and so embedded in our rebellious founding is the enslavement of millions of Africans and Indigenous people. In the 1700s and 1800s, there was abolition. There was the temperance movement. There were women's movements, including the suffrage movement.

We often don't consider how rebellious of a time the early days were. We had anarchists! We had women's suffrage! We had communists! We had presidents being assassinated and even more assassination attempts! From 1865–1901, Lincoln, Garfield, and McKinley were all killed. In 1909, there was a plot against Taft. In 1912, Teddy Roosevelt was shot. In 1928, there was a plot against Hoover. In 1933, a plot against FDR. As both fictional and nonfictional accounts of this time are beginning to emerge, I suggest spending some time contemplating how we moved from a world of ideological pluralism, to war, to the McCarthy era of closing the possibility of ideological diversity.

1950s/Early 1960s

In the post-war world of the 1950s, there was an attempt to exert social control, sending (middle class) women back into the home and away from job sites. McCarthyism hunted down communists and outliers.

Even so, there was no hope of keeping social rebellion quiet for long. An arts movement, marked in part by the Beats, emerged at the time, with writers like Jack Kerouac and poets like Allen Ginsberg exploring new ways of living.

In the United Kingdom, a group of documentarians began to interview children seven-year-old children in 1964 for the "Up Series," following their lives every seven years. Nine installments have been released to date; the most recent, "63 Up," aired in 2019.

In the meantime, various identity-based groups were beginning to gain momentum, like the Chicano movement that had begun in the 1940s as a Mexican-American rights movement. One activist with Chicano heritage traced their family's story of protest back to the 1960s where their parents participated in the east LA walkouts for Chicano rights. Of course, the civil rights movement had a profound effect on the consciousness of almost every activist I spoke with; because it's the only story we tell well, if incompletely, it has a powerful impact on the imaginations and aspirations of American activists.

Late 1960s/Early 1970s

As the Cold War heated up in the early 1960s, the world began to organize against the possibility of nuclear war. In early 1961, about 50,000 women marched across the country to demonstrate against the testing of nuclear weapons, the largest women's movement of the twentieth century. In June 1982, over 1 million people turned out in New York City to protest the nuclear arms race (my very first protest), echoed by millions marching in Western Europe as well.

The 1960s and 1970s were a rebellious time in the United States. In part, this is because of the Vietnam War. My father marched against the war, burned his draft card, and helped friends who were drafted escape to Canada. Activists I interviewed remembered marching against the war, and watching Walter Cronkite announce the war's costs on the nightly news. These protests heated up in 1968, and continued until the United States withdrew from the war in 1973.

In 1972, the Equal Rights Amendment (ERA) to the US Constitution passed both the House and the Senate, but then was not ratified by a sufficient number of states to become law. Many activists point to their work on the ERA, and then the bitter feeling when it failed to be ratified, as a galvanizing political moment.

In 1973, the Supreme Court ruled that women have a constitutional right to abortion in *Roe v. Wade.* This decision was overturned by activist judges appointed by Donald Trump shortly before its fiftieth anniversary.

In 1978, Václav Havel wrote "The Power of the Powerless;" the late 1970s and early 1980s would witness renewed protests against communism in Poland and the Czech Republic in particular, ultimately leading to the fall of communism beginning in 1989.

ACT UP, or the AIDS Coalition to Unleash Power, was formed in 1987 in New York City as a political action group to bright awareness to and to fight the AIDS crisis. ACT UP's use of street theater and disruptive protest techniques changed the course of modern American protest and forced the Reagan administration to begin to pay attention to the horrifying epidemic.[2]

1990s

In 1994, California voters passed the unconstitutional Prop 187, which prohibited undocumented immigrants from accessing public services like health care. A major immigrant rights movement, including members with ties to the Chicano movement, mobilized against the law and to support the lawsuit that challenged its constitutionality.

2000s

The September 11 attacks had a chilling effect on political activism in the country (instead bringing about a rally-around-the-flag effect— only Representative Barbara Lee voted against giving President Bush the authority to wage war). However, the violence against Muslim and Sikh Americans in the aftermath of the attacks provided an important impetus for organizing and advocacy on behalf of these groups.

In 2008, Barack Obama was elected, in part because of the social movements that galvanized to support him.

2010

From 2010–2012, anti-regime and pro-democracy protests swept across states in the Middle East and North Africa, called, optimistically, the Arab Spring.

Also in 2010, the Supreme Court decided in the hugely consequential Citizens United ruling that private organizations could spend virtually unfettered amounts of money on political campaigns, and that these donations were equivalent to free speech and so protected by the First Amendment. When you talk to progressive protesters, overturning Citizens United and getting money out of politics is high on their wish list.

2011

In 2011 the Occupy protests emerged across the country after originating in Zuccotti Park on Wall Street in New York City. The protesters demonstrated against neoliberalism and inequality; no one I interviewed claimed to be part of Occupy movements (though I had friends who joined them when I was in grad school at Rutgers during the time, and we sent pizza to the protesters a few times).

On opposite side of the country, the American Redoubt movement was forming based on the idea that conservative Christians should immigrate to the Northwest (Montana, Idaho, Wyoming).

2012

In 2012, 17-year-old Trayvon Martin was shot and killed by George Zimmerman as he walked through his neighborhood. Zimmerman, claiming self-defense, was acquitted. This shooting of an unarmed Black teenager became a foundational moment in the consciousness of many people I interviewed.

In August, there was a mass shooting at a gurdwara, a Sikh temple, in Oak Creek, Wisconsin, where six people were killed and four injured. This hate crime against people of the Sikh religion was galvanizing for Sikh activists I interviewed.

2014

Two years after Trayvon Martin was killed, 18-year-old Michael Brown was shot six times by a police officer named Darren Wilson in Ferguson, Missouri in August 2014. His body was left in the street for four hours. After this shooting, thousands of people traveled to Ferguson to protest police brutality against Black people.

In September 2014, Scotland held an independence referendum to vote on whether they would remain a part of the United Kingdom; the referendum failed with 55 percent of Scots voting to remain in the United Kingdom. Many Scots voted to stay because of the United Kingdom's membership in the European Union, which allowed them or their children to live and work anywhere in Europe.

2015

In 2015, Ireland, the birthplace of my maternal grandparents, became the first country to legalize gay marriage via national referendum after a stunning national campaign that set the stage for the abortion referendum a few years later.

2016

In February, Antonin Scalia died, leaving a rare vacancy on the Supreme Court in an election year where the president's party did not control the Senate (spoiler alert—this matters because it gives Republicans the votes to overturn *Roe v. Wade* in 2022). Obama nominated the mild-mannered Merrick Garland, but Mitch McConnell, the Senate Majority Leader, refused to give him a vote, holding the seat open for nearly a year until Trump became president and nominated Neil Gorsuch.

In June 2016, the United Kingdom voted to withdraw from the European Union; only Scotland and Northern Ireland voted to remain. The vote was close—51.9 percent voted to withdraw—and many compared it to the economic nationalist message espoused by Trump during the 2016 election here. The Brexit vote to withdraw from the EU, then, felt very much like a betrayal to many activists in Scotland who had organized on the "remain" side.

On November 8, 2016, Donald Trump was elected the forty-fifth president of the United States, losing the popular vote by 2.8 million (about 3 percent) but securing 306 electoral votes of the 270 needed to win. Republicans also gained control of the House and the Senate, giving them a governing trifecta for the next two years. There's no doubt that the election of 2016 reflected, on the one hand, the Tea Party/antiestablishment spirit on the right, and the "heritage of the immigrant rights movement, Occupy, and Black Lives Matter" on the left (Meyer & Tarrow, 2018).

As Bernie Sanders mounted his presidential run in 2016 and 2020, he was aided by his organizing branch, Our Revolution, which supported Bernie and then organized on the progressive economic issues he brought to political discourse.

2017

In January 2017, a Women's March was organized in Washington, DC, the largest protest in our nation's history. Hundreds of sister marches were held all over the world. Pink pussy hats became a sign of the resistance as a kind of callback to Trump's "grab them by the pussy" comment, although they were criticized for reifying feminism. We attended a surprisingly large march in Lincoln.

In late January, Trump issued Executive Order 13769, a "Muslim ban," restricting the travel of people from seven Muslim-majority countries (including Syrian refugees). Immigration lawyers rushed to airports to defend people en route to the United States as protests swelled outside international arrivals halls. Some of the earliest anti-Trump protests were against this ban, siding with the immigrants in their communities. My parents appeared on the Austin local news, holding signs welcoming immigrants. Lincoln and Omaha are thriving refugee resettlement communities, and so the news of the travel ban reverberated loudly through our town. We attended a vigil in Omaha, and I remember being so heartened by the number of people who turned out, and so frightened about what was going to come next. We ate Ethiopian food afterward, supporting a restaurant we loved that was run by a refugee family. I cohosted a teach-in at my university, where the largest classroom on campus was packed with students and faculty trying to understand what this meant for the future of foreign policy and immigration in our country. Even though the Women's March often, and deservedly, gets the spotlight for mobilizing people, we shouldn't sleep on the power of these early protests against the travel ban.

Donald Trump had campaigned on a platform of repealing the individual mandate for health insurance in the Affordable Care Act (which would effectively kill the legislation that relied on the individual mandate to achieve universal coverage). In July 2017, in a high-drama, late-night Senate session, John McCain broke with his party to vote against repealing the mandate, saving the ACA. This was a huge boon to Resistors, who had organized around saving the law and expanding health care access.

In August 2017, a Unite the Right rally took place in Charlottesville, Virginia. The rally was a gathering of supremacists angry at the proposed removal of a statue of Robert E. Lee. Thirty-two-year-old Heather Heyer, who was part of a counter protest against the rally, was murdered by a supremacist who ran over her with a car.

In 2006, sexual assault survivor and organizer Tarana Burke coined term "#MeToo," beginning a movement of women who spoke up about their history of sexual abuse and assault both at home and in the workplace. In 2017, the #MeToo movement became a global phenomenon as women began to talk publicly about their abuse, often from people in positions of great power.

In November 2017, Larry Krasner was elected District Attorney of Philadelphia. Krasner's election (and decisive reelection in 2021) was revolutionary because of his focus on criminal justice reform, including ending prosecution of marijuana offenses, ending cash bail, and reducing sentences. A Reclaim Philadelphia member I interviewed remarked, "Larry [Krasner] admits he wouldn't have been elected without Reclaim Philadelphia. We knocked on 30,000 doors. We went all out for him. We went back to our neighbors and talk to them again." When we attended a Reclaim Philadelphia meeting in South Philly, in 2018, one of the topics was the makeup of city council. Philly has a seat reservation system (kind of a quota system) where at least two seats are reserved for the party out of power—up until then, the seats had always been guaranteed to Republicans. City organizers decided that, instead, the Working Families party should contest those seats. In 2019, Kendra Brooks won one of those at large seats, and in 2023, Nicholas O'Rourke won the second. Organizing works.

2018

The year 2018 was an eventful one—hold on! In April 2018, Black Lives Matter planned the Black Women's March, which planned to march across the former Tappan Zee Bridge in New York to call attention to issues facing Black women. Police turned them away from the bridge. One person I interviewed helped to organize the march.

On Valentine's Day, a former student stormed into Marjory Stoneman High School in Parkland, Florida, killing 17 students with an assault rifle and injuring 17 others. The surviving Parkland students organized, and March For Our Lives was born. There were student-led protests throughout the country (I attended one in Lincoln), and over 500,000 people marched in Washington, DC.

When Bryan Stevenson, the lawyer who wrote the astounding book *Just Mercy* about his advocacy to defend people on death row, won the MacArthur "Genius" award, he decided to use the money to open Legacy Museum: From Enslavement to Mass Incarceration in Montgomery, Alabama, on the site of a former slave auction house. In 2018, when the museum opened, the Equal Justice Initiative hosted a Peace and Justice Summit. I attended, with my infant daughter and three students, and it was one of the most transformative experiences of my life. I spent two days listening to Black intellectuals and activists from Brittney Packnett to Michelle Alexander to Jelani Cobb to Catherine Flowers discuss the future of social justice in our country, from environmental racism (cohosted by a very funny Al Gore!) to the school to prison pipeline to mass incarceration. It was a singular moment in shaping my thinking about who was doing the work that this country needed to free itself.

Remember when small-but-mighty Ireland voted to legalize gay marriage? The rockstar activists didn't stop there, but instead turned their energy into a nationwide abortion referendum; in May 2018, 66 percent of the people in Ireland voted to legalize abortion in the country.

In June, the true scope of Trump's family separation policy of immigrants arriving at the border, spearheaded by the evil Stephen Miller, finally gained national attention. We learned that children were being separated from their parents, with no identifying information or plan for reunification. Those children were being locked in cages, sexually abused, trafficked, and experiencing tremendous trauma. As were their parents and caregivers. Families Belong Together protests shook the nation, galvanizing a multiyear protest to close the camps and reunite families. My brother Tommy, who had taken a job with the ACLU of Texas shortly after Trump was elected, was part of the legal team that represented detainees and their families. Justice moves slowly, and the following year the Families Belong Together protests were joined by another round of Close the Camps.

In August, students at UNC Chapel Hill held a "Remove Silent Sam" rally on campus. Silent Sam was a statue erected in 1913 as a monument to the confederacy. It stood in a position of honor at the front door to the university; although there were sporadic protests against the status throughout the twentieth century, in 2017 organized groups of undergraduate and graduate students began to agitate for its removal (my brother Ben was part of several of these, and was pepper-sprayed by police while protesting). Finally, the students were able to bring the statue down, a major victory for groups across the country fighting to remove confederate monuments from positions of prestige.

The Proud Boys, a far-right militia group with ties to the Trump administration, continued to gain traction, turning up at anti-Trump protests and instigating violence, including against members of antifa. The rise and normalization of these anti-establishment, highly armed groups of course reached their crescendo (for now) in 2021 during the January 6 insurrection, but they were major instigators of political violence early on. Many of them were jailed.

In 2018, Justice Kennedy resigned from the SCOTUS, and Trump nominated Brett Kavanaugh to fill this seat. Christine Blasey

Ford, a psychology professor, testified in front of the Senate Judiciary Committee that Kavanaugh had sexually assaulted her at a party when they were in high school. There was intense pressure from the left for Trump to withdraw the nomination and appoint someone without a sketchy financial background and a credible accusation of sexual assault, but those didn't seem to be sticking points, and the Senate voted to confirm Kavanaugh in October 2018.

In the November midterms, Democrats won back the House, effectively shutting down the legislative power of the Republicans for the remaining two years of Trump's term. It was considered a Blue Wave; Democrats won the popular vote in the House by about 10 million votes, the largest midterm margin for either party. It was the highest voter turnout in a midterm election since 1914. Some people think that anger over the Kavanaugh confirmation, in part, was what drove the Blue Wave.

One other major outcome of the midterms were ballot referenda in Idaho and Nebraska to expand Medicaid, huge victories in traditionally red states.

While the good people of Ireland were putting their energy toward making change, on our shore we got to meet our very own BBQ Becky, a woman who called the cops on a Black family in her neighborhood who were—wait for it—having a cookout.

In the meantime, men who were part of the protests against Michael Brown's death in Ferguson continued to die in suspicious circumstances, including being found in torched cars and three alleged suicides that family members believed were actually murders.

2019

By 2019, the American Redoubters had not only elected at least two politicians in Idaho, but also were patrolling the highways and putting up checkpoints, looking for protesters. Several of my participants significantly changed their protest strategy because American Redoubt was circulating their photos.

2020

In early 2020, the COVID pandemic began, which had tremendous effects on activism and organizing.

In May 2020, George Floyd, a Black man in Minneapolis, Minnesota, was murdered by Derek Chauvin, a police officer, who knelt on his neck for nine minutes. After the video of George Floyd's murder went viral, a month of protests swept the country in what Tanisha called "the uprising."

As protests swept the United States in June 2020, JK Rowling was leading a brave battle of her own: for the right to discriminate against transgender folk. Yes, JK Rowling came out as a TERF. As did the Nigerian-American author (who I've read, and loved) Chimamanda Adichie. Ugh, you people!

On September 18, 2020, Ruth Bader Ginsburg died of pancreatic cancer at the age of 87, breaking the heart of every progressive woman in America (my older daughter's middle name is Ruth). Trump nominated and confirmed Amy Coney Barrett, who drew comparisons to *The Handmaid's Tale,* in record time, and sealed the fate of abortion rights in our country.

In the September presidential debate with Joe Biden, Trump, when asked about political violence, supremacist, and militia groups, told the Proud Boys to "stand back and stand by," which many people took as a sign that he would give them the signal to move. He also secretly had COVID there, which he gave to Chris Christie during debate prep, and could have also given to Joe Biden.

In October, the FBI announced a domestic terror plot to kidnap Gretchen Whitmer, the democratic governor of Michigan, organized by rightwing militia members. This underscored how dangerous those on the right had become.

In November 2020, Joe Biden defeated Donald Trump in the election for the forty-sixth president of the United States. Like Trump in 2016, Biden won 306 electoral votes; Biden also won about 7 million more votes in the popular count than Trump.

I'm sure you remember BBQ Becky from 2018; in 2020 a woman named Karen called the cops on a man birdwatching with his dog in Central Park. In her honor, *The Guardian* declared 2020 the "Year of the Karens."

2021

On January 6, 2021, I was turning 40 and my son was turning seven. My attention was torn between the unwrapping of birthday gifts and my Twitter feed, which was documenting in real time a siege on our nation's capital. "What the fuck is happening?" I tried to whisper to my husband. "Mom! Don't swear during cake time!" Sorin admonished me.

Zooming out from our own celebration, January 6, 2021, was an armed insurrection in the Capitol Building of the United States to stop Joe Biden's electoral victory from being certified. The militias wanted to hang Mike Pence, who refused to go along with the insane plan to decertify the election.

Property was destroyed, and police officers were killed, injured, and risked their lives as they diverted protesters, likely saving the lives of members of Congress and their staff.

That evening, the results of Georgia's dual Senate runoff elections were announced. Both Rafael Warnock and Jon Ossoff had won, giving Democrats a trifecta in the House, Senate, and executive branch. It was a wild day. (I got an Apple Watch. Sorin got Legos.)

2022

In 2022, the Varieties of Democracy group, which tracks democratic and authoritarian trends worldwide, warned that the United States was on the verge of losing its status as a liberal democracy. The report's authors wrote: "Liberal democracy remains significantly lower than before Trump came to power. Government misinformation declined last year but did not return to previous levels. Toxic levels of polarization continue to increase. Democracy survives in the United States, but it remains under threat. Of all the forces undermining democratic traditions in elections and policymaking—Donald Trump's big lie, the politicization of ballot counting by Republican state legislatures, the attempt to disenfranchise segments of the population—one that has devastating potential is operating under the radar: the growing cynicism of younger voters."

After Republicans lost control of the federal government, Republican-controlled state houses began to pass a variety of "anti-woke" bills (bleh) on the state level, mostly targeting kids. These included anti-trans bills, prohibiting kids from playing sport with kids who are the gender they identify with, anti-CRT bills, which are nebulous enough to ban teaching most race-related topics in public schools, and Florida's famous "Don't Say Gay" law, which prohibits discussion of gay people in public schools.

In 2022, the Supreme Court of the United States overturned *Roe v. Wade* in the Dobbs decision, triggering a wave of anti-abortion laws across the country. At last, Mitch McConnell could see his effort of stealing the Supreme Court seat from Merrick Garland come to fruition. In response, the 2022 midterms were the best for a ruling party in history with Democrats keeping control of the Senate and only narrowly losing the House. A series of statewide votes followed, either to protect the right to abortion or to ban abortion on the state level; around two-thirds of voters consistently voted to protect abortion in these races.

At the People's Choice Awards in 2022, Lizzo was given the award of People's Champion. She used this platform to recognize the work of 17 activists around the United States, from trans rights activists to anti-gun organizers to abortion-rights activists. Lizzo said in her acceptance speech: "To be an icon isn't about how long you've had your platform. Being an icon is about what you do with that platform. Ever since the beginning of my career, I've used my platform to amplify marginalized voices."

Although this is obviously an imperfect summary of activism in this country, hopefully it gives you a flavor of how many stories are told about protest, how deeply they're woven into who we are as a nation. We're a country of resisters and rebels. It's time to burn some things down, or at least turn up the heat a little bit.

Un-Ban the Books:

READING TO HELP YOU GET SMARTER

Republicans wouldn't be so determined to keep books away from people if they didn't know how powerful a good book can be. Use this QR code to check out a list of books that will help you get smarter—download the list, pass it around, and let me know what else should be on it.

Here are some that can help you get smarter. Read one, pass the list along, and add to it. This list is incomplete, and by the time this book is in your hands there will be another hundred books challenging us to reimagine protest. But this can get you started.

A NOTE ON THE RESEARCH DESIGN IN THIS BOOK

First, an apology of sorts. When I started this work back in 2017, my goal was very simple: I was going to chronicle four years of protests, and then publish this, like my first book, as an academic monograph. Of course, over the four years, things got wonky. There was a pandemic. I had my third kid. I got tenure, and realized that Nebraska was not a good place for our family. I realized that I didn't just want to chronicle protests, but rather create a book that would be helpful (and funny and authentic) to people trying to *engage* in activism. But the book has deep roots in academia, because I have deep roots in academia. So I fear at times I've created something at once illegible to nonacademics and at the same time unsatisfying to academics. If this is true, the fault is entirely mine. This is likely most true in the endnotes, where I weave in both snarky commentary and also the scholarly backbone and context of the book. If that feels dizzying, well . . . that's is what it is like in my head.

I have also adapted the reference style to fit the tone of the book in a way that I hope is legible, with apologies to *The Chicago Manual of Style* and my proofreaders. Here's the method behind my madness: There is a "further reading" section for each chapter, where I suggest some podcasts, newspapers, or magazine articles related to the current events I'm writing about. These are only referenced in the text when I directly quote or paraphrase from them. For scholarly sources, I use a modified endnote style. When I have more to say about a particular topic, I put the reference in the endnote itself. If I'm quoting or paraphrasing but don't have anything more to say, I save myself (and you) the hope of finding some witty commentary and just put the reference in the text. I tried very, very hard to credit everyone whose intellectual history informed this book and am very happy to answer questions if you have them.

I did the interviews with approval from Nebraska Wesleyan University's Internal Review Board, which guarantees certain protections to people who participate in academic research. This is really different from journalistic ethics, which frown, for the most part, on "unnamed sources." As I said in the introduction, I blinded the participants by 500 miles and gave them pseudonyms because of what I perceived to be my ethical obligations. I did, however, triangulate information that participants shared with me, independently verifying facts that are available in the public record. And since I'm not making generalizable claims, just sharing stories that were told to me, I think that the words of the participants speak for themselves.

This book features the voices of 44 activists, with in-depth profiles of nine interwoven throughout the book. Activists are truly some of the best people in America. These folks are deeeep into zoning debates, becoming policy wonks so they can lobby city council on budgetary line items. But they're also dispensing clean needles in the community. They're creating the fabric of mutual aid, passing out flashlights and warm blankets during power outages. They're on the frontlines for trans rights and reproductive freedom. I spent four years talking to them, finding out what made them tick. Here's how I did it: In all, 111 total interviews were conducted with 44 participants; 25 participants completed all three rounds of interviews in 2018, 2019, and 2020 (56 percent). Seventy percent of my initial cohort participated in either the second or third round of interviews; 6 of 44 (13 percent) declined to be interviewed again or were unable to be contacted after the first round of interviews, and two kept in touch with me informally but never completed another interview.

For the ones did talk with me, our relationship grew close over the course of this research. They asked me to put them in touch with each other activists, asked if I knew folks working on these side issues. They gave me books to read, sent me their material, ran slogans by me. More than one cried during our conversations. I wasn't always sure when they would call, so I did interviews in cars, in the parking lot of IKEA, in the back bedroom at my parent's house.

Stage one: To get a picture of the organizing landscape in all 50 states, I sent a survey in spring 2018 to all Indivisible chapters in cities with over 200,000 people and the biggest city in states with no cities above 200,000. For each of these cities, I also targeted Black Lives Matter, labor, and immigration groups. I asked questions about organizational strategies, including issue priorities, recruitment strategies, and effective means of mobilization. 196 participants responded to the survey from every state except for Delaware (why, Delaware?).

Stage two: In summer 2018, I conducted semi-structured interviews with 44 participants. Of these, 38 had completed the survey and volunteered to do interviews, and eight were referrals from interview participants. The interviews asked questions about their history of activism, how the individual and group were focused on local/state/national issues, how they were organizing, and perceived challenges or divides within the progressive political community in their area.

Stage three: I also conducted midterm interviews, on the phone and via email, in winter 2018 and summer 2019, for a total of 31 interviews.

Stage four: In September 2020, I sent emails to the 44 participants. I conducted interviews with 31 activists and conducted a post-election follow-up with five, for a total of 36 interviews.

I also did ethnographic work from 2017–2020 as a participant-observer at over 25 activism and organizing events in all regions of the United States, from protests to town hall meetings to strategy sessions in living rooms and bars.

SCHOLARLY WORKS CITED

Abramowitz, A., & McCoy, J. (2019). United States: Racial Resentment, Negative Partisanship, and Polarization in Trump's America. *The ANNALS of the American Academy of Political and Social Science, 681*①, 137–156.

Ai, W. (2021). *1000 Years of Joys and Sorrows: A Memoir*. Bond Street Books.

Albert, J. C., & Albert, S. E. (1984). *The Sixties Papers: Documents of a Rebellious Decade*. Praeger Books.

Alexander, M. (2012). *The New Jim Crow: Mass Incarceration in the Age of Colorblindness*. The New Press.

Andrews, K. T., Caren, N., & Browne, A. (2018). Protesting Trump. *Mobilization: An International Quarterly, 23*④, 393–400.

Ash, T. G. (2014). *The Magic Lantern: The Revolution of '89 Witnessed in Warsaw, Budapest, Berlin and Prague*. Atlantic Books Ltd.

Baker, J. E., & Clancy, K. A. (2020). "Scoping" the Routes, Roots, and Rights to the City: "Mobilities of Vision" and Reading the Social Movement Landscape of Thessaloniki, Greece. *GeoHumanities, 6*②, 252–279.

Baker, J. E., Clancy, K. A., & Clancy, B. (2020). Putin as Gay Icon? Memes as a Tactic in Russian Lgbt+ Activism. *LGBTQ+ activism in Central and Eastern Europe: Resistance, representation and identity*, 209–233.

Baldwin, J. (1963). *The Fire Next Time*. Dial Press.

Baldwin, J. (2012). *Notes of a Native Son*. Beacon Press.

Barkan, A. (2019). *Eyes to the Wind: A Memoir of Love and Death, Hope and Resistance*. Atria Books.

Bauer, K., & Clancy, K. (2018). Teaching Race and Social Justice at a Predominantly White Institution. *Journal of Political Science Education, 14*①, 72–85.

Baumgardner, J., & Richards, A. (2005). *Grassroots: A Field Guide for Feminist Activism*. Macmillan.

Berger, P. L., & Luckmann, T. (1991). *The Social Construction of Reality: A Treatise in the Sociology of Knowledge*. Penguin UK.

Berry, M., & Chenoweth, E. (2018). Who Made the Women's March? *The Resistance: The Dawn of the Anti-Trump Opposition Movement*, 75–89.

Betts, P., & Betts, P. (2010). 1736 Socialism's Social Contract: Individual Citizen Petitions. In *Within Walls: Private Life in the German Democratic Republic* (pp. 0). Oxford University Press. https://doi.org/10.1093/acprof:oso/9780199208845.003.0007

Bevins, V. (2023). *If We Burn*. Hachette Publishing Group.

Bonilla, T., & Tillery, A. B. (2020). Which Identity Frames Boost Support for and Mobilization in the# Blacklivesmatter Movement? An Experimental Test. *American Political Science Review*, 114④, 947–962.

Butorac, S. K. (2018). Hannah Arendt, James Baldwin, and the Politics of Love. *Political Research Quarterly*, 71③, 710–721.

Campbell, D. E. (2013). Social Networks and Political Participation. *Annual Review of Political Science*, 16, 33–48.

Campbell, T. (2021). Black Lives Matter's Effect on Police Lethal Use-of-Force. *Available at SSRN*.

Carvan, T. (2022). *This Is Not a Book About Benedict Cumberbatch: The Joy of Loving Something—Anything—Like Your Life Depends on It*. GP Putnam's Sons.

Chemaly, S. (2018). *Rage Becomes Her*. Simon and Schuster.

Chenoweth, E. (2016, Nov 21). People Are in the Streets Protesting Donald Trump. But When Does Protest Actually Work? *Washington Post*. https://www.washingtonpost.com/news/monkey-cage/wp/2016/11/21/people-are-in-the-streets-protesting-donald-trump-but-when-does-protest-actually-work/

Chenoweth, E. (2021). *Civil Resistance: What Everyone Needs to Know®*. Oxford University Press.

Coates, T.-N. (2015). *Between the World and Me*. Spiegel & Grau.

Cohen, E. L., Forbis, M. M., & Misri, D. (2018). Introduction: Protest. *WSQ: Women's Studies Quarterly*, 46③, 14-27.

Cooper, B. (2018). *Eloquent Rage: A Black Feminist Discovers Her Superpower*. St. Martin's Press.

Cormack, Lindsey (forthcoming). *How to Raise a Citizen (And Why It's Up to Us to Do It)*. Jossey Bass.

Crimp, D., & Rolston, A. (1990). *Aids Demo Graphics*. Bay Press Seattle.

Davary, B. (2016). #Black Lives Matter. *Ethnic Studies Review*, 37–38(11).

Davis, A. Y. (2016). *Freedom Is a Constant Struggle: Ferguson, Palestine, and the Foundations of a Movement*. Haymarket Books.

deBoer, F. (2023). *How Elites Ate the Social Justice Movement*. Simon and Schuster.

Della Porta, D. (2020). *How Social Movements Can Save Democracy: Democratic Innovations from Below*. John Wiley & Sons.

Della Porta, D., & Diani, M. (1999). *Social Movements: An Introduction*, Blackwell.

Della Porta, D., & Felicetti, A. (2019). Innovating Democracy against Democratic Stress in Europe: Social Movements and Democratic Experiments. *Representation*, 1–18.

Diani, M. (2004). Networks and Participation. *The Blackwell Companion to Social Experiments*, 339-359.

Dreier, P. (2008). Will Obama Inspire a New Generation of Organizers? *Dissent*.

Dworkin, A. (2006). *Heartbreak: The Political Memoir of a Feminist Militant*. Bloomsbury Publishing.

Einwohner, R. L., Kelly-Thompson, K., Sinclair-Chapman, V., Tormos-Aponte, F., Weldon, S. L., Wright, J. M., & Wu, C. (2019). Active Solidarity: Intersectional Solidarity in Action. *Social Politics: International Studies in Gender, State & Society*.

Engler, M., & Engler, P. (2016). *This Is an Uprising: How Nonviolent Revolt Is Shaping the Twenty-First Century*. Bold Type Books.

Enikolopov, R., Makarin, A., & Petrova, M. (2016). Social Media and Protest Participation: Evidence from Russia.

Filindra, A. (2023). *Race, Rights, and Rifles: The Origins of the NRA and Contemporary Gun Culture*. University of Chicago Press.

Fisher, D. R., Jasny, L., & Dow, D. M. (2018). Why Are We Here? Patterns of Intersectional Motivations across the Resistance. *Mobilization: An International Quarterly, 23④*, 451–468.

Ford, P. K., Johnson, T. A., & Maxwell, A. (2010). "Yes We Can" or "Yes We Did"? Prospective and Retrospective Change in the Obama Presidency. *Journal of Black Studies, 40③*, 462–483.

Forman, M. (2010). Conscious Hip-Hop, Change, and the Obama Era. *American Studies Journal, 54*.

Forna, A. (2003). *The Devil That Danced on the Water*. Grove Press.

Garza, A. (2020). *The Purpose of Power: How We Come Together When We Fall Apart*. One World.

Gessen, M. (2014). *Words Will Break Cement: The Passion of Pussy Riot*. Penguin.

Gilmore, R. W. (2007). *Golden Gulag: Prisons, Surplus, Crisis, and Opposition in Globalizing California* (Vol. 21). Univ of California Press.

Giridharadas, A. (2022). *The Persuaders: At the Front Lines of the Fight for Hearts, Minds, and Democracy*. Knopf.

Giroux, H. (2009). Youth and the Myth of a Post-Racial Society under Barack Obama. *Policy Futures in Education, 7⑤*.

Glaser, B. G. (2002). Constructivist Grounded Theory? *Forum qualitative sozialforschung/forum: Qualitative social research*.

Goldstone, J. (2003). *States, Parties, and Social Movements*. Cambridge University Press.

Goodwin, J., & Jasper, J. M. (2006). Emotions and Social Movements. In *Handbook of the Sociology of Emotions* (pp. 611–635). Springer.

Goodwin, J., Jasper, J. M., & Polletta, F. (2004). Emotional Dimensions of Social Movements. *The Blackwell Companion to Social Movements*, 413–432.

Goodwin, J., Jasper, J. M., & Polletta, F. (2009). *Passionate Politics: Emotions and Social Movements*. University of Chicago Press.

Goodwin, J., & Pfaff, S. (2001). Emotion Work in High-Risk Social Movements: Managing Fear in the Us and East German Civil Rights Movements. *Passionate politics: Emotions and social movements, 2001,* 282–302.

Gorski, P., Lopresti-Goodman, S., & Rising, D. (2019). "Nobody's Paying Me to Cry": The Causes of Activist Burnout in United States Animal Rights Activists. *Social Movement Studies, 18③,* 364–380.

Gosa, T. L. (2010). Not Another Remix: How Obama Became the First Hip-Hop President. *Journal of Popular Music Studies, 22④,* 389–415.

Gose, L. E., & Skocpol, T. (2019). Resist, Persist, and Transform: The Emergence and Impact of Grassroots Resistance Groups Opposing the Trump Presidency. *Mobilization: An International Quarterly, 24③,* 293–317.

Gould, D. B. (2009). *Moving Politics*. University of Chicago Press.

Graham, M. H., & Svolik, M. W. (2020). Democracy in America? Partisanship, Polarization, and the Robustness of Support for Democracy in the United States. *American Political Science Review, 114②,* 392–409.

Green, D. (2016). *How Change Happens*. Oxford University Press.

Hale, H. E. (2013). Regime Change Cascades: What We Have Learned from the 1848 Revolutions to the 2011 Arab Uprisings. *Annual Review of Political Science, 16,* 331–353.

Hannah-Jones, N. (2021). *The 1619 Project: A New American Origin Story.* Random House.

Harris, J., & Davidson, C. (2009). Obama: The New Contours of Power. *Race & Class, 50④,* 1–19.

Hasan, M. (2023). *Win Every Argument: The Art of Debating, Persuading, and Public Speaking*. Henry Holt and Co.

Hassell, H. J., Holbein, J. B., & Baldwin, M. (2020). Mobilize for Our Lives? School Shootings and Democratic Accountability in Us Elections. *American Political Science Review, 114④,* 1375–1385.

Havel, V. (2009). *The Power of the Powerless (Routledge Revivals): Citizens against the State in Central-Eastern Europe*. Routledge.

Hayes, K., & Kaba, M. (2023). How Much Discomfort Is the Whole World Worth? *Boston Review.* https://www.bostonreview.net/articles/how-much-discomfort-is-the-whole-world-worth/?fbclid=IwAR2jaib h1TbVElRfGYmo7zP1h66wKiWZzS_XpAQa5b8PbgSXnYkYXylL8ko.

Hayes, K., & Kaba, M. (2023). *Let This Radicalize You: Organizing and the Revolution of Reciprocal Care*. Haymarket Books.

Hayward, C. R. (2020). Disruption: What Is It Good For? *The Journal of Politics, 82*②, 448–459.

Heaney, M. T., & Rojas, F. (2015). *Party in the Street: The Antiwar Movement and the Democratic Party after 9/11*. Cambridge University Press.

Hoffman, A. (2021). *Steal This Book*. Hachette UK.

Hooker, J. (2016). Black Lives Matter and the Paradoxes of U.S. Black Politics: From Democratic Sacrifice to Democratic Repair. *Political Theory, 44*④, 448–469.

hooks, b. (2000). *All About Love: New Visions*. William Morrow Paperbacks.

Hunt, S. A., & Benford, R. D. (1994). Identity Talk in the Peace and Justice Movement. *Journal of Contemporary Ethnography, 22*④, 488–517.

Hunt, S. A., & Benford, R. D. (2004). Collective Identity, Solidarity, and Commitment. *The Blackwell Companion to Social Movements, 433*(57).

Hunt, S. A., Benford, R. D., & Snow, D. A. (1994). Identity Fields: Framing Processes and the Social Construction of Movement Identities. *New Social Movements: From Ideology to Identity, 185*, 208.

Ishizuka, K. (2016). *Serve the People: Making Asian America in the Long Sixties* Verso Books.

Jackson, S. J. (2016). (Re) Imagining Intersectional Democracy from Black Feminism to Hashtag Activism. *Women's Studies in Communication, 39*④, 375–379.

Jaffe, S. (2016). *Necessary Trouble: Americans in Revolt*. Bold Type Books.

Jobin-Leeds, G. (2016). *When We Fight, We Win: Twenty-First-Century Social Movements and the Activists That Are Transforming Our World*. The New Press.

Johnson, A. E., & Wilkinson, K. K. (2021). *All We Can Save: Truth, Courage, and Solutions for the Climate Crisis*. One World.

Johnson, D., & Merians, V. (2017). *What We Do Now: Standing up for Your Values in Trump's America*. Melville House.

Jones-Eversley, S., Adedoyin, A. C., Robinson, M. A., & Moore, S. E. (2017). Protesting Black Inequality: A Commentary on the Civil Rights Movement and Black Lives Matter. *Journal of Community Practice, 25*(3-4), 309–324.

Kaba, M. (2021). *We Do This Til We Free Us: Abolitionist Organizing and Transforming Justice* (Vol. 1). Haymarket Books.

Kaplan, L. (2019). *The Story of Jane: The Legendary Underground Feminist Abortion Service*. University of Chicago Press.

Kaur, V. (2020). *See No Stranger: A Memoir and Manifesto of Revolutionary Love*. One World.

Kendi, I. X. (2012). *The Black Campus Movement: Black Students and the Racial Reconstruction of Higher Education, 1965–1972*. Springer.

Kendi, I. X. (2023). *How to Be an Antiracist*. One World.

Kreiss, D. (2012). Acting in the Public Sphere: The 2008 Obama Campaign's Strategic Use of New Media to Shape Narratives of the Presidential Race *Research in Social Movements, Conflicts and Change, 33*, 195–223.

LaDuke, W. (1999). *All Our Relations: Native Struggles for Land and Life*. South End Press.

Larreboure, M., & González, F. (2019). The Impact of the Women's March on the Us House Election.

Lee, F. L., Chan, M., & Chen, H.-T. (2020). Social Media and Protest Attitudes During Movement Abeyance: A Study of Hong Kong University Students. *International Journal of Communication, 14*, 20.

Levin, E., Greenberg, L., & Padilla, A. (2016). Indivisible: A Practical Guide for Resisting the Trump Agenda. *Retrieved November, 1*, 2022.

Levin, S. A., Milner, H. V., & Perrings, C. (2021). The Dynamics of Political Polarization. In (Vol. 118, pp. e2116950118): National Acad Sciences.

Lewis, K., Gray, K., & Meierhenrich, J. (2014). The Structure of Online Activism. *Sociological Science, 1*, 1–9.

Light, M., & Light, K. (2020). *Picturing Resistance: Moments and Movements of Social Change from the 1950s to Today*. Ten Speed Press.

Lim, C. (2008). Social Networks and Political Participation: How Do Networks Matter? *Social Forces, 87②*, 961–982.

Lipsitz, R. (2022). *The Rise of a New Left: How Young Radicals Are Shaping the Future of American Politics*. Verso Books.

Lowery, W. (2016). *They Can't Kill Us All: Ferguson, Baltimore, and a New Era in America's Racial Justice Movement*. Hachette UK.

Maerz, S. F., Lührmann, A., Hellmeier, S., Grahn, S., & Lindberg, S. I. (2020). State of the World 2019: Autocratization Surges–Resistance Grows. *Democratization, 27⑥*, 909-927.

Marsden, P. V., & Campbell, K. E. (2012). Reflections on Conceptualizing and Measuring Tie Strength. *Social Forces, 91①*, 17–23.

McAdam, D., & Tarrow, S. G. (2010). Ballots and Barricades: On the Reciprocal Relationship between Elections and Social Movements. *Perspectives on Politics, 8②*, 529–542.

McGhee, H. (2022). *The Sum of Us: What Racism Costs Everyone and How We Can Prosper Together*. One World.

McQuiston, L. (2019). *Protest!: A History of Social and Political Protest Graphics*. Frances Lincoln.

Meyer, D. S., & Tarrow, S. (2018). *The Resistance: The Dawn of the Anti-Trump Opposition Movement*. Oxford University Press.

Morales-López, E., & Floyd, A. (2017). *Developing New Identities in Social Conflicts: Constructivist Perspectives* (Vol. 71). John Benjamins Publishing Company.

Mundt, M., Ross, K., & Burnett, C. M. (2018). Scaling Social Movements through Social Media: The Case of Black Lives Matter. *Social Media+ Society*, 4④, 2056305118807911.

Nafisi, A. (2008). *Reading Lolita in Tehran: A Memoir in Books*. Random House Trade Paperbacks.

Nagoski, E., & Nagoski, A. (2020). *Burnout: The Secret to Unlocking the Stress Cycle*. Ballantine Books.

Paine, T. (1776). *Common Sense: 1776*. Infomotions, Incorporated.

Papada, E., Altman, D., Angiolillo, F., Gastaldi, L., Köhler, T., Lundstedt, M., Natsika, N., Nord, M., Sato, Y., & Wiebrecht, F. (2023). Defiance in the Face of Autocratization. Democracy Report 2023. *Democracy Report*.

Parastou Forouhar: Art, Life and Death in Iran. (2011). (R. Issa, Ed.)

Passy, F. (2001). Socialization, Connection, and the Structure/Agency Gap: A Specification of the Impact of Networks on Participation in Social Movements. *Mobilization: An International Quarterly*, 6②, 173–192.

Payne, C. M. (2007). *I've Got the Light of Freedom: The Organizing Tradition and the Mississippi Freedom Struggle*. Univ of California Press.

Pearlman, W. (2018). Moral Identity and Protest Cascades in Syria. *British Journal of Political Science*, 48④, 877–901.

Pettinicchio, D. (2019). *Politics of Empowerment: Disability Rights and the Cycle of American Policy Reform*. Stanford University Press.

Ransby, B. (2018). *Making All Black Lives Matter: Reimagining Freedom in the Twenty-First Century* (Vol. 6). Univ of California Press.

Reed, T. F. (2018). Between Obama and Coates. *Catalyst*, 1④.

Reny, T. T., & Newman, B. J. (2021). The Opinion-Mobilizing Effect of Social Protest against Police Violence: Evidence from the 2020 George Floyd Protests. *American Political Science Review*, 115④, 1499–1507.

Roca, B., & Díaz-Parra, I. (2021). Spatial Perspectives on Labor and Social Movements: Multidisciplinary Dialogues and Dilemmas. *Sociology Compass*, 15①, e12845.

Rose-Redwood, C., & Rose-Redwood, R. (2017). 'It Definitely Felt Very White': Race, Gender, and the Performative Politics of Assembly at the Women's March in Victoria, British Columbia. *Gender, Place & Culture*, 24⑤, 645–654.

Rosenbaum, S., & Talmor, R. (2022). Self-Care. *Feminist Anthropology*, 3②, 362–372.

Rothstein, R. (2017). *The Color of Law: A Forgotten History of How Our Government Segregated America*. Liveright Publishing.

Saint-Exupéry, A. d. (1943). *The Little Prince*. Reynal & Hitchcock.

Scott, J. C. (2010). *The Art of Not Being Governed: An Anarchist History of Upland Southeast Asia*. Nus Press.

Scott, J. C. (2012). *Two Cheers for Anarchism: Six Easy Pieces on Autonomy, Dignity, and Meaningful Work and Play*. Princeton University Press.

Setzler, M., & Yanus, A. B. (2018). Why Did Women Vote for Donald Trump? *PS: Political Science & Politics, 51*③, 523–527.

Shapiro, J. P. (1994). *No Pity: People with Disabilities Forging a New Civil Rights Movement*. Crown.

Sharlet, J. (2008). *The Family: The Secret Fundamentalism at the Heart of American Power*. HarperCollins.

Sharp, G. (1973). The Politics of Nonviolent Action, 3 Vols. *Boston: Porter Sargent, 2*.

Shepherd, L. L. (2023). *Resistance from the Right: Conservatives and the Campus Wars in Modern America*. University of North Carolina Press.

Shore, M. (2018). *The Ukrainian Night*. Yale University Press.

Skocpol, T. (2019). Making Sense of Citizen Mobilizations against the Trump Presidency. *Perspectives on Politics, 17*②, 480–484.

Smith, C. (2021). *How the Word Is Passed: A Reckoning with the History of Slavery across America*. Hachette UK.

Smith, L. (1994). *Killers of the Dream*. WW Norton & Company.

Smith, S. (2018). *Subterranean Fire: A History of Working-Class Radicalism in the United States*. Haymarket Books.

Snow, D., Benford, R., McCammon, H., Hewitt, L., & Fitzgerald, S. (2014). The Emergence, Development, and Future of the Framing Perspective: 25+ Years since" Frame Alignment." *Mobilization: An International Quarterly, 19*①, 23–46.

Snow, D. A., & Benford, R. D. (1988). Ideology, Frame Resonance, and Participant Mobilization. *International Social Movement Research, 1*①, 197–217.

Snow, D. A., & Benford, R. D. (2005). Clarifying the Relationship between Framing and Ideology. *Frames of Protest: Social Movements and the Framing Perspective, 205*, 209.

Stevenson, B. (2015). *Just Mercy: A Story of Justice and Redemption*. One World.

Taylor, K.-Y. (2017). *How We Get Free: Black Feminism and the Combahee River Collective*. Haymarket Books.

Taylor, V., & Van Dyke, N. (2004). 'Get Up, Stand Up:' Tactical Repertoires of Social Movements. In S. A. S. David A. Snow, Hanspeter Kriesi (Ed.), *The Blackwell Companion to Social Movements* (pp. 262–293).

Thunberg, G. (2023). *The Climate Book: The Facts and the Solutions*. Penguin.

Tien, C. (2017). The Racial Gap in Voting among Women: White Women, Racial Resentment, and Support for Trump. *New Political Science, 39*④, 651–669.

Tilly, C. (2002). *Stories, Identities, and Political Change*. Rowman & Littlefield.

Traister, R. (2023). *Good and Mad: The Revolutionary Power of Women's Anger*. Simon and Schuster.

Treuer, D. (2019). *The Heartbeat of Wounded Knee: Native America from 1890 to the Present*. Penguin.

Tufekci, Z. (2017). *Twitter and Tear Gas: The Power and Fragility of Networked Protest*. Yale University Press.

Vargas, J. A. (2018). *Dear America: Notes of an Undocumented Citizen*. HarperCollins.

Walker, H. L. (2020). Targeted: The Mobilizing Effect of Perceptions of Unfair Policing Practices. *The Journal of Politics, 82*①, 119–134.

Weyland, K. (2019). Why Some Democracy Protests Do Diffuse. *Journal of Conflict Resolution, 63*(10), 2390–2401.

White, M. (2016). *The End of Protest: A New Playbook for Revolution*. Knopf Canada.

Windschitl, M. (2002). Framing Constructivism in Practice as the Negotiation of Dilemmas: An Analysis of the Conceptual, Pedagogical, Cultural, and Political Challenges Facing Teachers. *Review of Educational Research, 72*②, 131–175.

Woodly, D. R. (2021). *Reckoning: Black Lives Matter and the Democratic Necessity of Social Movements*. Oxford University Press.

Young, R. (2015). *Dissent: The History of an American Idea*. NYU Press.

Yurchak, A. (2013). *Everything Was Forever, until It Was No More: The Last Soviet Generation*. Princeton University Press.

CHAPTER NOTES

Introduction

1   For a global introduction to civil resistance, I highly recommend Chenoweth (2021).

2   Now is a good time to open the playlist if you need a little bit of Bowie while you read this chapter.

3   For a fascinating view of how long Republicans have been organizing like this, see Lauren Lassabe Shepherd's fabulous book *Resistance from the Right*.

4   And we need to avoid the forced choices that the media narrative constantly tries to impose. In 2023, when the horrifyingly sad war between Israel and Hamas began, my social media feed began to organize itself into apologists for Netanyahu and apologists for Hamas. Most of the people I talked to in the world outside of social media were turned off by both sides, and avoiding the debate at all costs. We can believe that people aren't their governments and that every civilian death is a tragedy for the world. I loathe Russia's invasion of Ukraine, and I grieve for the people killed by Putin's horrendous war every day. And yet my heart still breaks when I see the numbers of Russian soldiers—many of them just boys—who have died for Putin's idiocy. In the same way, the life of an Israeli baby is worth the same as the life of a baby in Gaza. We have to be able to see both things as true.

5   Erica Chenoweth and colleagues at the Crowd Counting Consortium published frequent updates of the size of protest crowds at anti-Trump events in the now-defunct *Washington Post* column "The Monkey Cage." See also Arnold et al., 2018; Berry & Chenoweth, 2018.

6   Researchers have overwhelmingly found that racial resentment was the major motivator behind White votes for Trump, including why women voted for Trump instead of Clinton (Abramowitz & McCoy, 2019; Setzler & Yanus, 2018; Tien, 2017).

7   You probably remember when Joe Biden famously told Obama, "This is a big fucking deal," and of course in some ways it was and still is. But as anyone who has tried to buy insurance on the marketplace will tell you, the fact that the country has done nothing to strengthen Obamacare since it passed has

continued to benefit insurers and not too many other people. We need, of course, universal health care.

8   In terms of books and their nonsubjects, I highly recommend Tabitha Carvan's *This is Not a Book About Benedict Cumberbatch*. This book is so funny in its critique of the way we treat girls and women and dismiss the things they love, and in a way that will catch you completely off guard. It reminds me of the amazing scene in Rebecca Makkai's *I Have Some Questions for You*, where she describes the freedom of rowing crew away from boys. "Even when the boys rowed past us, all we'd do was holler or chant; we didn't have to drop everything to watch them, which was the usual expectation." Later in the chapter, the narrator concludes, "At the time, what rankled was the idea that we were supposed to see these boys as the starts, to fall at their sweaty feet. What bothers me now is those boys internalizing girls as audience, there only to act as mirrors, to make their accomplishments realer." Lord if that doesn't describe most of my adolescence.

9   See appendix for more on how the research got done.

10   If you have never watched the excellent *Up* documentary series, you should. The series follows 14 individuals from across Britain, beginning in 1964 with *Seven Up!* when the participants were 7 years old (and then follows *14 Up!* in 1971, *21 Up!* in 1978, and so on, spanning 56 years. Michael Apted, the director, pledged only to contact the participants every seven years, which was broken only to attend Bruce's wedding after *42 Up*.

11   I independently confirmed each of these with local media reports of protests. I don't provide links to these stories to protect the identity of my participants as much as possible, but if you google "violence against protesters" you'll see that it's not an anomaly.

12   Sorry, Dad.

13   Progressivism, liberalism, leftism, socialism . . . as Alfred says in *Miracle on 34th Street*, "all the -isms." I'm using progressivism, broadly, to mean what I describe in Step One: a radically inclusive, multiracial, socialist democracy.

14   The Proceedings of the National Academy of Sciences recently ran an entire issue dedicated to understanding polarization (Levin et al., 2021).

15   And this isn't true only in the United States: this kind of targeted oppression of women is seen throughout autocratic regimes, as Chenoweth and Marks (2022) show—and Chenoweth's forthcoming book promises to further explore.

16   I feel like a more masterful writer would have a whole slew of chess puns here. Clinton is no one's queen! The electoral college is a bunch of pawns! Someone stop me.

17   Of course, the war Russia is waging against Ukraine is not the first time that Ukrainians have fought for democracy, as Marci Shore's *The Ukrainian Night* illustrates through interviews with activists who were part of the Maidan protests. The book asks the most chilling question of all: what is worth dying for?

Step One

1 Of course, this is an homage to Karl Marx's "A spectre is haunting Europe—the spectre of communism." One of the great lines in music from the early 2000s is from the White Stripes' "Little Ghost," which I can't quote because of copyright, but I snuck onto the playlist so you can get it stuck in your head.

2 For more discussion about the relationship between democratization and social movements see Della Porta (2020).

3 As Graham and Svolik (2020) find, *revealed* preferences for democracy also aren't as robust as *expressed* preferences—that is, people are "In a sharply polarized electorate, even pro-democratically minded voters may act as partisans first and democrats only second." Put another way, people may say that they value democracy, but that only goes as far as siding with their party goes. This is also messy because, right now, both parties think there is a democratic crisis, but there are deeply divergent reasons why.

4 And there is certainly a reciprocal relationship between elections and movements, and I'd even argue that the past few election cycles have muddied what those boundaries between the two are (Kreiss, 2012). However, the important thing is that activism can't stop at the ballot box (McAdam & Tarrow, 2010).

5 I'm married to a geographer, so I know that maps are political. And also, the Gall-Peters projection scene is one of the all-time great moments in *The West Wing*.

6 Now is a good time to open the playlist and put on "Fixed Positions" by Andrew Bird.

7 In the United States, we've seen democratic participation and social movements (though not innovation) that scholars think are key to improving participatory democracy (Della Porta & Felicetti, 2019).

8 I was interviewed for this fantastic article by Marin Cogin, explaining how women changed their life choices in response to *Dobbs*. https://www.vox.com/culture/23559583/roe-abortion-dobbs-reproductive-rights

9 Interestingly, the pro-Palestinian protests that happened in the wake of Israel's invasion of Gaza were bigger from its inception than the pro-*Roe v. Wade* protests were at their peak. It's not always predictable when, and why, people choose to turn out. By far, the best source for tracking size and composition of protests is the Crowd Counting Consortium, which makes their data available online and writes a lovely blog to help us make sense of, well, everything.

10 I'd like to thank Dr. Daphne Penn for this formulation.

11 Szalai (2023) does a nice job of reviewing books that offer differing views of inequality and how to fix it; it's impossible to read this without noticing how economic issues cannot be solved without attention to social issues.

There are, obviously, whole books to be written about the evils of neoliberalism. You may remember the heartbreaking death in 2013 of Mary

Vojtko, an adjunct professor at Duquesne, who died after she could no longer access health insurance because her contract wasn't renewed. My friend Amy tells a story of visiting a university in the Bay Area, and asking a friend about the rows of RVs and cars on the shoulder of the road. These belonged to other professors who couldn't afford housing in the area, so they slept in their cars and then commuted to work.

12   See Lindsey Cormack's great new book *How to Raise a Citizen (And Why It's Up to Us to Do It)* for a close look at why civics instruction in this country needs to change. Also see Dispatch 20 for the latest in the coordinated attack against civics instruction.

13   James Baldwin is perhaps the preeminent thinker in terms of the politics of love (Hooker, 2016); It's useful I think to problematize here the way that theorists have helped understand love in a political context. For example, philosopher Hannah Arendt had an enormous amount of trouble seeing the logic in Baldwin's insistence on love in politics: however; for Baldwin, love was at the core of his believe that America could actualize its democracy: love is a driving force not to accept things as they are, but to create a more perfect union (Butorac, 2018). Similarly, Arendt spars with Ralph Ellison over the wisdom of sending Black children into dangerous situations to integrate schools (mistakenly believing that this is driven by self-interest). Instead, Hooker (2016) argues that here, Arendt misunderstands the nature of the Black families' motivations: they aren't having their children be the face of integration because of self-interest, but rather as community sacrifice, to bring on a better future for everyone.

14   In late 2023, Poland defeated their Trump-aligned PiS party. They are now doing the hard work of rebuilding a flourishing democracy, and it's not easy.

15   The organizing in Wisconsin over the past several years, and cooperation between organizers and the progressive wing of the party, has been a masterclass in getting shit done #Protasiewicz.

16   See Heaney and Rojas (2015). And, although it's worth reading everything she writes, but here it's also worth revisiting Francis Fox Piven's article "Occupy! And Make Them Do It: Elections and Movements Don't Proceed on Separate Tracks."(Piven, 2012)

17   The people who write about religion and capitalism probably get a lot right. Here I'm thinking of Jeff Sharlet's *The Family* in particular.

18   Her son Jordan was shot as he played loud music in his car at a gas station in 2012. Her congressional website, and most speeches, refer to her most important job as "Jordan's mom." This world will break your heart.

19   I'm not giving you a link to MAGA rap! That you need to find on your own.

20   Obama was the first (and certainly, for now, the last) hip-hop president. In one song, listeners are encouraged to "Barack the Vote," and in another to "Go tell ya' mama [to] vote for Obama." What's not to love (Gosa, 2010)? It didn't hurt that his workout playlist had Beyoncé and Jay-Z on it (Forman, 2010), or that the paparazzi caught him shirtless in Hawaii so you could *see* that he worked

out. These things were obviously helpful in creating youth support around his candidacy (Giroux, 2009).

21   I don't have enough fingers and toes to count the number of people who have told me they are avoiding conversations about Gaza because of the propensity of the left to eat their own. The internet these days seems to foreclose the possibility for nuanced conversation.

22   Kelly Hayes and Mariame Kaba (2023). Also see their new book, *Let this Radicalize You* (K Hayes & M Kaba, 2023), and of course Kaba's foundational book *We Do This Til They Free Us* (Kaba, 2021).

23   Our daughter's middle name is Ruth, named for Ruth Bader Ginsburg. We also have a very cozy throw pillow with RBG's likeness on it. She tells everyone that she was named after her favorite pillow.

24   Need more proof that young people are the way? Check out *The Rise of a New Left* (Lipsitz, 2022).

Further Reading for This Chapter

The Monkey Cage (https://www.washingtonpost.com/monkey-cage/), in conjunction with the crowd counting consortium, published consistent counts of crowd sizes at protests throughout the Trump administration. You can see the data here (https://sites.google.com/view/crowdcountingconsortium/home).

Baldwin, J. (1979) James Baldwin Writing and Talking. *The New York Times*.

Chait, J. (2016). Five Days That Shaped a Presidency: Barack Obama Shares with Jonathan Chait a Very Early Draft of His Memoirs. *New York Magazine*.

Domonoske, C. (2023). UAW Auto Strike: What To Know About The Big 3 Automakers And The Union. *NPR*. https://www.npr.org/2023/10/06/1204233323/uaw-auto-strike-big-3-automakers-union-shawn-fain

Engbar, D. (2023). How We Turned the Tide in the Roach Wars. *The Atlantic*. https://www.theatlantic.com/podcasts/archive/2023/11/cockroach-bait-invention-combat/676167/

Ludden, J. (2016). How Politics Killed Universal Child Care In The 1970s. *All Things Considered*. https://www.npr.org/2016/10/13/497850292/how-politics-killed-universal-childcare-in-the-1970s

Mack, D. (2020). Why are Journalists Always Visiting Diners in Trump Country? *The Counter*. Accessed February 4, 2024. https://thecounter.org/trump-rust-belt-diner-presidential-race-election-2020/

Mack, K, and Palfray, J. Capitalizing Black and White: Grammatical Justice and Equity. MacArthur Foundation. Accessed February 4, 2024. https://www.macfound.org/press/perspectives/capitalizing-black-and-white-grammatical-justice-and-equity

Piven, F. F. (2012). Occupy! And Make Them Do It: Elections and Movements Don't Proceed on Separate Tracks. *The Nation* (April 2). https://www.thenation.com/article/occupy-and-make-them-do-it/s

Stolberg, S.G. How Turned Off Are Voters? Check Out Tommy's Diner. *The New York Times*. October 15, 2016. https://www.nytimes.com/2016/10/15/us/ohio-voters-trump-clinton.html

Szalai, J. (2023). Economists Ignored Inequality for Years. Now They Can't Stop Talking About It. *The New York Times*.

Whalen, Jeanne. (2023). UAW, GM Sign Tentative Deal that Will End Strike if Workers Ratify It. *The Washington Post*. washingtonpost.com/business/2023/10/30/gm-uaw-tentative-agreement/

Step Two

1   The Women's March was so successful at organizing because of its deep network of groups that fed into the march; this also helped those networks stay activated and connected once the march was over. As two prominent social movements scholars wrote: "A growing consciousness has emerged that these struggles are interrelated; that racial justice is related to economic justice and climate justice, for instance. Indeed the national co-chairs of the Women's March cut their teeth in community organizing in forming coalitions and solidarity networks across their organizational affiliations" (Berry & Chenoweth, 2018, p. 78).

2   Tilly (2002)—this book is so great for seeing the way that stories mediate conflict and change, from the Zapatista rebellion to conflicts with White nationalists.

3   Twitter, now lovingly known as X, served this function until 2022. It was a place where people could listen and learn from other groups without having them go through the labor of teaching. I learned a lot, for instance, from following the conversations of activists with disabilities about the issues they confront, particularly through COVID. It remains to be seen what might take the place of Twitter in this way.

4   I attended the summit; these observations are from my notes and personal recollection of the event. Michelle Alexander is, most notably, the author of *The New Jim Crow*. Sherrilyn Ifill is the president and director-council for the NAACP's Legal Defense Fund, and Jelani Cobb is a journalism professor at Columbia and a writer for *The New Yorker*. This panel had a major impact on my thinking about race.

5   Della Porta (2020) finds that, historically, "movements on behalf of excluded groups often cooperated and learned from each other." We see this kind of cooperation between the abolitionist movement in the US and the UK, which had major impacts on other types of activism, including women's rights and women suffrage. At the beginning of the twentieth century, labor movements cooperated with women suffrage movements as well.

6   Researchers who study mobilization try to explain when and how people opt to participate in collective action. These include instrumentalist/rationalist explanations that focus on when people have incentives to participate (money, status, power, etc), social constructivist explanations that focus on the role that

identity and symbols can play in inspiring people to mobilize, and networking explanations that focus on how different connection matters. (See, for example, Campbell, 2013; Della Porta & Diani, 1999; Diani, 2004; Lim, 2008; Marsden & Campbell, 2012).

Weak ties are just as effective at recruiting activists for major protests, but that neighborhood/community ties are most effective in recruiting local community activists (Lim 2008). Movements grow out of existing networks, and provide social identities for their participants. They also plug members into opportunities for action and decision-making (Passy, 2001); social media is obviously particularly adept at creating loose ties that provide opportunities for action and for pooling groups of volunteers (Enikolopov et al., 2016; Kreiss, 2012; Lee et al., 2020; Lewis et al., 2014; Mundt et al., 2018).

7   Sidney Tarrow, one of the most prominent scholars of protest, argues that there are three criteria for taking a one-off event like the Women's March and turning it into a durable cycle of mobilization—amplification, scale shifting, and spillover (Meyer & Tarrow, 2018). In other words, the message of the march needs to travel beyond the protesters themselves into diffuse networks and across the media to be *amplified*, global issues need to become localized and local issues globalized to be relevant to different audiences as the *scale shifts*, and there needs to be a *spillover* of issues as the focus of protest broadens. All three of these happened in the months following the Women's March, aided in part by the work of groups like Indivisible. Additionally, women's rights and reproductive rights were common issues that "serve as a bridge between different social issues and movements" (Fisher et al., 2018). These are sometimes called WUNC displays (it's fun to say - just try it): they demonstrate the movement's worthiness, unity, numbers, and commitment.

8   This is important because there is a cyclical nature to protest in this country: "By revitalizing and legitimating the social movement form, the civil rights movement of the early 1960s reintroduced . . . centrifugal pressures to American politics. Or more accurately, it was one movement—civil rights—and one powerful countermovement—white resistance . . . that began to force the parties to weigh the costs and benefits of appealing to the median voter against the strategic imperative of responding to mobilized movement elements at the ideological margins" (Meyer & Tarrow, 2018, pp. 10–11).

9   Not reading Harry Potter to your kids is an act of resistance. At the very least, buy it used.

10   Skocpol also engages in an interesting conversation about the blinders we have about who "should" be at the helm of progressive movements. Researchers and the public often think that movements are exclusively led by "young people and persons of color with leftist views." What was interesting about the anti-Trump resistance was that it was, in fact, a movement of mostly White females, not all of whom are progressive. Gose and Skocpol (2019) characterize the movement as such: "Today's female-led, anti-Trump resistance represents a 21st-century reincarnation and updating of longstanding female citizen activism in American democracy." There are real impacts to a movement being led by mostly

well-to-do White women, including the way that identity is performed in protest spaces and marches (Rose-Redwood & Rose-Redwood, 2017).

11   Allyship is complicated, and often deeply intertwined with questions of identity. The book comes back again and again to the idea that you often need to give up your own privilege in order for broader expressions of solidarity—but also how hard that really is. Cohen et al. (2018) reflect on the contrast of groups that organized after Trump: "The 2017 women's marches in the United States, where viral internet photographs of police officers in pussy hats smiling with women marchers contrasted sharply with the images (and indeed the reality) of riot police confronting Black Lives Matter protesters and #NoDAPL water protectors—a reminder that racialized subjects are the ones least likely to be perceived as legitimate protesters, by the state or the general public." The major question of how to protect the marginalized and disempowered members of the coalition is a vital one.

12   I had a few different quotes from the luminary Audre Lorde here, and kept taking them out. One quote, "If they cannot love and resist at the same time, they probably will not survive," circulates quite a bit, but it's out of context: she's speaking about motherhood. The beginning of the quote is this: "*Raising Black children—female and male—in the mouth of a racist, sexist, suicidal dragon is perilous and chancy.*" Without coopting Lorde's deep work on parenting for my own purposes, I will say that her formulations on survival have been important as I thought through this book. And the fact that she shares a birthday with Toni Morrison means that the universe's sense of humor, at times, is kind.

13   After Fetterman had a stroke on the campaign trail, it became clear that he needed captions because processing vocalized speech was difficult for him. He movingly explained in various interviews how the stress of recovering from major surgery while running for office in one of the country's most high-stakes elections created the conditions for him to be institutionalized with depression shortly after his election.

Further Reading for This Chapter

Alexander, M. (2018). We Are Not the Resistance. *The New York Times*. https://www.nytimes.com/2018/09/21/opinion/sunday/resistance-kavanaugh-trump-protest.html

Crouch, I. (2014, March 12). Obama Wins on "between Two Ferns." *The New Yorker*. https://www.newyorker.com/culture/culture-desk/obama-wins-on-between-two-ferns

Ludden, J. (2016) How Politics Killed Universal Child Care In The 1970s. *All Things Considered, NPR News*, Accessed February 4, 2024. https://www.npr.org/2016/10/13/497850292/how-politics-killed-universal-childcare-in-the-1970s

Millhiser, I. (2023). The Unconstitutional Plan to Stop Women from Traveling out of State for an Abortion, Explained. *VOX*,. https://www.vox.com/23868962/texas-abortion-travel-ban-unconstitutional

Obamagirl. "I have a crush on Obama." YouTube video. Accessed February 4, 2024. https://www.youtube.com/watch?v=wKsoXHYICqU

Robinson, M. (2015, November 5). President Obama & Marilynne Robinson: A Conversation in Iowa. *New York Review of Books*. http://www.nybooks.com/articles/2015/11/05/president-obama-marilynne-robinson-conversation/

The West Wing. Gall-Peters Projection, season 2, episode 16.

Zenko, Micah. (2016). Obama's Embrace of Drone Strikes Will Be A Lasting Legacy. *The New York Times*, https://www.nytimes.com/roomfordebate/2016/01/12/reflecting-on-obamas-presidency/obamas-embrace-of-drone-strikes-will-be-a-lasting-legacy

Step Three

1   Also feminist triumphs: *Desk Set, Mary Poppins, Miracle on 34th Street* (I published a whole article about this for a now-defunct media outlet, but the text is on my website). I'll put the politics of those movies against *Love Actually* or *Bridget Jones's Diary* any day.

2   On the absence of bravery, we just need to look to the international community's willingness to allow genocide to proceed in Gaza. In February 2024, Brazilian president Lula condemned the international community cutting off aid to the Palestinians, saying "we need to stop being small when we need to be big."

3   In a heartbreaking episode of Pod Save the World, Ben Rhodes recounts his relationship with Navalny, musing that rage, humor, and family were what kept him alive.

4   Of course, Navalny is a complicated figure, as Masha Gessen's excellent profile in *The New Yorker* suggests (https://www.newyorker.com/news/our-columnists/the-evolution-of-alexey-navalnys-nationalism). He without question held, at least at early points in his career, racist views toward immigrants and Central Asian migrants. It's not clear to me (as a non-historian/expert) how much those views evolved over the course of his life. But we can hold two ideas in our heads at the same time: be in awe of Navalny's willingness to sacrifice his life to resist authoritarianism, and also that we should hold leaders to the high standard of resisting racism. We can do both.

5   Organizing nonviolent civil resistance is also the focus of Erica Chenoweth's 2022 book.

6   Feminist social movement scholars can also help us understand these moments. Cohen et al. (2018) remind us that looking at expressions of activism beyond protest is both politically and empirically wise: "We must also be aware of those resisters whose bodies cannot be at the protest march for multiple reasons, not limited to precarious labor, citizenship status, the prison-industrial complex, and disability." Activists were not only people who showed up for marches, but those who engaged in the behind-the-scenes analysis of movement-making . . . the quiet work that goes into building contention is itself a feminist enterprise. By looking at mobilization and protest in this more expansive way we can also "trace activism from the streets to the statehouse," realizing that it has to occur lots of places (Fisher et al., 2018). This allows us

to explore the "fuzzy and permeable boundary between institutionalized and noninstitutionalized politics" (Goldstone, 2003). As Della Porta (2020, p. 164) writes, "In these times, as backlashes are visible, there is, however, also space for agency on the side of the progressive actors. In fact, these are times of risks but also of chances."

7   If you don't already have it open, maybe it's time for "Just a Girl" on the playlist for Step Three.

8   I believe I heard Barack Obama use the term "confined by anger," but I cannot find the reference. If you know it, email me!

9   A text I received while phone banking once. Message received!

10 Remember Susan Zhuang, my now-city council member? In one of her first acts after being elected, she organized a huge rally against opening a family shelter in our neighborhood.

11 I read broadly, have eclectic friends, and generally feel like more is more in terms of the rich variety of life. Give me a new country to explore over an old favorite. Let's try that new momo place! (But not pizza—there's only one pizza place worth eating out in South Brooklyn, and that's Rob's). There is a lot of music I like listening to, but given my druthers, the only music I will put on Spotify when I am alone is Andrew Bird (and Neutral Milk Hotel's album "In the Aeroplane Over the Sea," the occasional Christmas album, and some Ani DiFranco throwback. Taylor Swift for some energy. You don't want to share Spotify with me.). The only concerts I willingly buy tickets to are Andrew Bird concerts. It completely checks off the "music" box in my brain. I imagine this is what it is like to be a single-issue activist: that the issue is enough for you in terms of activating both your emotion and your intellect to keep you completely engaged and to cede the rest of the world of being angry to other people.

12 I mean, Donald Trump did tell Mark Milley to "just shoot" protesters during the George Floyd protests, so we're not far off. In May of 2024, Greg Abbott pardoned a vigilante who had shot and killed a protester during a Black Lives Matter demonstration. In April 2024, the Supreme Court ruled that a police officer injured in protests in Baton Rouge could sue civil rights activist DeRay Mckesson just for organizing the protests. They're coming for your right to organize.

13 Only tangentially related, but perhaps worth a mention, is the rich global history of underground and alternative education pathways that people create when the government tries to suppress knowledge—the Flying University in Poland (and the secular homeschooling movement in the United States) are two of many examples.

14 These are called cascade effects, or protest diffusion, or contagion effects in different literatures. See, e.g., (Hale, 2013; Pearlman, 2018; Weyland, 2019).

15 So then, why was there only anemic protest activity, at best, post-*Dobbs*? I have a theory that people tend not to protest when they think the president agrees with them but I'm still trying to puzzle this out myself. And yet 40 percent of

Americans and 62 percent of liberals told Gallup that they were motivated to protest in 2022.

16   Just like Obama! There's a lot of great work that's been done about Obama's ties to organizing in Chicago, how he used his skills and his connections from his activist background to run for Senate and then president, and his at times acrimonious relationship with the Movement for Black Lives and other activist groups during his presidency. See, for starters (Crouch, 2014; Dreier, 2008; Fausset, 2015; Ford et al., 2010; Harris & Davidson, 2009; Morgan, 2017; Reed, 2018; Robinson, 2015).

17   Which has the reputation, if not actually the numbers, to call itself a global protest leader.

18   Frank Sinatra once threatened to punch a journalist in the mouth for suggesting he wore a hairpiece. If you don't believe this is true, that little things can get under the skin of politicians, look only to Putin's ban on depictions of him in drag. People are so sensitive! (Baker et al., 2020). Trump's relentless attacks on the appearances of his foes . . . autocrats know that they have no depth, so become thin-skinned and image obsessed. Use that to your advantage.

19   Hooker (2016) argues that overemphasizing nonviolence gets complicated and ignores the fact that there are real moments when violence might be the only way out of a situation.

20   Poor Kavanaugh was just trying to enjoy a nice, quiet steak dinner at Morton's . . .

21   Elon Musk too! How much money can one billionaire spend to force strangers to pay attention to him?

22   Disruption can "interrupt privileged people's motivated ignorance" (Hayward, 2020, p. 449) because, as Frances Fox Piven says so nicely, "elites depend on the masses to cooperate in agenda-setting schemes" (451). In other words, they think you'll back down—call that bluff.

23   In order to create a sense of discomfort, disruption is key. Jackson (2016) notes that Black activists today are increasingly willing to "interrupt and take up space in the political and cultural places that have too long included them only if they willingly remain at the margins." In other words, disruption and coalition building have managed to get intersectional politics as part of the cultural mainstream. Bonilla and Tillery (2020) call BLM the first "avowedly intersectional movement to gain significant traction in the American public sphere."

24   If we can stay in that general part of the world for a second, there's another great book by Alexei Yurchak called *Everything Was Forever, Until It Was No More,* which explores the symbols and cultural practices of the final Soviet generation before the incredible collapse of the USSR. Read this synopsis and tell me it doesn't apply to the US, if not in substance, than at least in spirit: "To the people who lived in that system the collapse seemed both completely unexpected and completely unsurprising. At the moment of collapse it suddenly became obvious that Soviet life had always seemed simultaneously eternal and stagnating, vigorous and ailing, bleak and full of promise. Although these

characteristics may appear mutually exclusive, in fact they were mutually constitutive" (Yurchak 2013).

25 You can think we're harsh, but in our house that applies to *Paw Patrol* and, sadly, *Mercy Watson* too.

26 James Scott is one of the more fascinating thinkers of our time. In *The Art of Not Being Governed*, he talks about how the upland folks of southeast Asia (the people of the Zomia) went through drastic cultural shifts like changing languages and "forgetting" how to write in order to maintain their independence from nation-states that wished to consolidate territory (his theory has been critiqued by some as painting the people Zomia as "primitive"). In *Two Cheers for Anarchism* (Scott, 2012), one of my favorite books to teach, he gives examples of what an anarchist approach to dissent, work, and play might look like: "I am making a case for a sort of anarchist squint. What I aim to show is that if you put on anarchist glasses and look at the history of popular movements, revolutions, ordinary politics, and the state from that angle, certain insights will appear that are obscured from almost any other angle."

27 And although COVID cut down on grocery store trips and lunch dates, it did not stifle protest. And although mask-free MAGA rallies like Sturgis became superspreader events, protests for Black lives did not.

28 In *Rucho v. Common Cause*, No. 18-422, and *Lamone v. Benisek*, No. 18-726, the Supreme Court ruled 5-4 that partisan gerrymandering was a political, rather than constitutional, issue (Liptak, 2019). In other words, let Congress and state legislatures decide.

29 My husband would like me to share with you this song by The Gate 5, which sets the text of this speech to lovely harmonization. We believe it's only available in WFMU's vault: http://blogfiles.wfmu.org/HT/Gate_5_-_Unknown.mp3

30 Allyship, however, can be hard, and needs to be conditional; groups are often hurt by "well-meant but ill-conceived gestures of solidarity" (Cohen et al., 2018). As Einwohner et al. (2019) note: "While solidarity lies at the heart of collective action, it is not easily achieved. Social movements are characterized not only by difference within activist ranks but also by power asymmetries that reflect broader domination and distrust." How to manage those, especially within a relatively diffuse situation, is a real that is at the heart of this book.

31 Obama deported 2.7 million people, over half of whom had no criminal record, betraying his pledge to focus on "felons not families" (Gonzalez, 2017; Milman et al., 2017).

32 This was quoted in Gonzalez (2017); also, *Sofia Valdez, Future Prez* is one of our favorite books in the Ada Twist series for kids.

33 Even if protests have an impact on public opinion and issue salience, on (some) subjects that's not enough to translate into electoral salience (e.g. shootings don't bring about electoral movement on the issue) (Hassell et al., 2020). A recent study of political attitudes before and after protest found that large scale protests did increase public support for those issues. These effects have also been found as a result of the George Floyd protests: there was an

opinion-mobilizing effect, even among those that didn't participate in the protests (Reny & Newman, 2021). However, this was only found among liberal and nonprejudiced Americans—conservative and high-prejudice Americans, unsurprisingly, remained unmoved. Quantitative data finds that the Women's March had an impact on underrepresented candidates running for office, their vote share, and number of citizens who turned out to vote: (Larreboure & González, 2019). While negative interactions with the state (like police brutality or being arrested) usually result in pulling back from political engagement, in some cases a kind of counternarrative emerges: "Narratives of injustice recast individual grievances in terms of structural inequality and indicate a group with whom to organize, laying the groundwork for action" (Walker, 2020).

Further Reading for This Chapter

Folmar, Chloe. (2022). "Morton's Condemns Abortion Rights Protesters for Disrupting Kavanaugh's Freedom to 'Eat Dinner.'" *The Hill*, July 8, 2022. https://thehill.com/regulation/court-battles/3549907-mortons-condemns-abortion-rights-protestors-for-disrupting-kavanaughs-freedom-to-eat-dinner/

Gonzalez, S. (2017). No One Expected Obama Would Deport More People Than Any Other U.S. President. *WNYC News*. https://www.wnyc.org/story/no-one-thought-barack-obama-would-deport-more-people-any-other-us-president/

Liptak, A. (2019). Supreme Court Bars Challenges to Partisan Gerrymandering. *New York Times*. https://www.nytimes.com/2019/06/27/us/politics/supreme-court-gerrymandering.html

Milman, O., et al (2017). Obama's Legacy: The Promises, Shortcomings and Fights to Come. *The Guardian*. https://www.theguardian.com/us-news/2017/jan/03/barack-obama-president-legacy-policy-issues-wins-fights

Morgan, D. F. (2017). Obama and Black Lives Matter: An Epilogue. *Al Jazeera* Retrieved January 27, from https://www.aljazeera.com/indepth/opinion/2017/01/obama-black-lives-matter-epilogue-170126073428660.html

Natanson, H. (2023). Objection to Sexual, LGBTQ Content Propels Spike in Book Challenges. *The Washington Post*, https://www.washingtonpost.com/education/2023/05/23/lgbtq-book-ban-challengers/.

Pengelly, M. (2021). Trump Told Top US General to 'Just Shoot' Racism Protesters, Book Claims. *The Guardian*.

Ziebell, J. (2022). Queer and Trans Prison Voices: A Podcast Archive on Prison Abolition. https://cuny.manifoldapp.org/projects/queer-and-trans-prison-voices

Zimmerman, J. (2017). The Monstrous Female Ambition of the Harpy. *Catapult*, https://catapult.co/stories/role-monsters-harpy-women-ambition

Step Four

1   Now is a good time to pull up "Cities" by Talking Heads on your playlist! (Somewhat in jest, but the song does a fantastic job of musing about what makes—and doesn't make—a community worth living in.)

2   As this great essay by Emily Raboteau illustrates, schools in NYC can very much be litmus tests of inequality. https://www.newyorker.com/books/page-turner/new-york-playgrounds-i-have-known

3   There's a lot of great work to read about why racism means we can't have nice things; in particular, the fact that desegregation led to integration of pools, which meant that racist White folks decided to defund public pools and flee to country clubs instead. Heather McGhee's (2022) *The Sum of Us* is a great place to start to get smarter about the history of divesting in communities.

4   One of my favorite memories of this happened during one of our trips to Greece, where a pro-LGBTQI march found us talking with a merry band of genderqueer anarchists who sold us some very nice homemade soap (Baker & Clancy, 2020).

    But a very fair question to ask after reading this section is: "How is this different from White flight to the suburbs?" and it's a question I struggle with *all the time*. One answer is that it isn't that different. We used our resources and privilege to opt out (financial, familial, flexible working schedules . . .) On the other hand, there is a profound *ideological* difference, I think, between wanting to drain resources from public goods in order to shelter your wealth, and wanting everyone to be taxed more so that the public goods that exist are *worth* participating in. Things are complicated, and people make decisions in contingent, fraught circumstances.

5   Donna della Porta describes how, during the pandemic, activist groups in Europe created the kind of mutual aid that stripped down, liberal states couldn't sustain: "So progressive civil society organizations and grassroots neighborhood groups distributed food and medicines, produced masks and medical instruments, given shelter to the homeless and protected women from domestic violence" (Della Porta, 2020).

6   There have been a *lot* of books lately about how to sway people who disagree with you. Anand Giridharadas's *The Persuaders* and *Win Every Argument* are two good ones; in my reading, it's hard to find books that don't devolve into a kind of coddling of racists: people are racist because they're not *heard*. We have more in common with racists than we know—we just need to give them *space*. The whole NYT diner theory of American politics. My take is that we should absolutely be open to having conversations with people who are curious, but otherwise we shouldn't feed the trolls.

7   In fairness, a *lot* of the activists I spoke with talked about creating space to engage with Trump voters. And I believe it's our job to try to organize the people in our own communities, so we are responsible for Uncle Bob and Aunt Ginny and their racism! I am just not convinced that the evidence supports trying to

engage people who support Trump so much as trying to talk with people in the middle.

8   Framing is the context in which a policy issue is placed in order to persuade people (Snow et al., 2014; Snow & Benford, 1988, 2005; Taylor & Van Dyke, 2004)—for example, activists framed universal health care as a moral issue talking to religious audiences, and an economic issue when talking to fiscally conservative audiences.

9   Conservative-leaning Staten Island, which is part of my congressional district, has been clear about its interest in seceding from New York City, giving up the only thing that makes it cool. A 2024 budget report found that secession would cost the good people of Staten Island millions of dollars a year in lost revenue from the city, so I suspect they'll stick around a while.

10   There is a rich body of literature on the relationship between emotions and activism (Goodwin et al., 2004, 2009; Goodwin & Pfaff, 2001).

11   This book has largely painted a positive image of organizing, but there is also the utterly cynical and political side too. Organizations accused of embezzling, or mishandling, money. People fought and dissolved their relationships. I don't know enough to take sides, or tell you how to avoid it, but it is a real reason that people threw up their hands and thought "welp, everyone's problematic, so why bother."

12   Burnout is also a major issue; as Gorski et al. (2019) found three major causes of burnout: 1) intrinsic motivational and psychological factors, 2) organizational and movement culture, and 3) within-movement in-fighting and marginalization.

13   Indeed, there were also suicides by active members the BLM community, causing activists and scholars to call for an investigation into suicide and suicide ideation in the activist community (Jones-Eversley et al., 2017).

14   A wealth of scholarship looks at the relationship between narratives and emotions—see, e.g., (Berger & Luckmann, 1991; Glaser, 2002; Hunt & Benford, 1994, 2004; Hunt et al., 1994; Morales-López & Floyd, 2017; Roca & Díaz-Parra, 2021; Windschitl, 2002).

15   There's a lot of great literature on self-care as a tool of neoliberal domination. If you want to get mad about self-care, read some of it (Rosenbaum & Talmor, 2022).

Further Reading for This Chapter

The Combahee River Collective Statement. https://americanstudies.yale.edu/sites/default/files/files/Keyword%20Coalition_Readings.pdf

France, D. (2020). The Activists. *The New York Times*. https://www.nytimes.com/interactive/2020/04/13/t-magazine/act-up-aids.html

Larson, S. (2018). "The Wilderness," Reviewed: Can a Partisan Podcast Save the Democratic Party? *The New Yorker*, July 25. https://www.newyorker.com/culture/podcast-dept/the-wilderness-reviewed-can-a-partisan-podcast-save-the-democratic-party

Pod Save America (November 9, 2023) "Major Win for Democrats, Minor Debate for Republicans." https://podcasts.apple.com/us/podcast/major-win-for-democrats -minor-debate-for-republicans/id1192761536?i=1000634225467

Conclusion and After Party

1   Game theory uses logic to predict what rational actors will do in a series of repeated interactions given potential costs and benefits of different decisions.

2   Even JD Vance, the author-turned-MAGA senator from Ohio, thinks so! https:// thehill.com/homenews/senate/4300013-jd-vance-ohio-abortion-vote/ I think often about how my entire university was compelled to read *Hillbilly Elegy* and Vance was invited to campus in 2016 to "explain" how "real America" felt, only to become one of the smarmiest senators around—which isn't easy to do!

1   Of course so much of our country's heartbreaking history is told through song. Can I suggest Childish Gambino's "This is America" (and the video especially) to start?

2   An earlier footnote recommended Rebecca Makkai's *I Have Some Questions for You.* Also great is her book *The Great Believers,* which does a lot of things but takes seriously the protests to bring visibility to the AIDS epidemic in the 1980s. The book is stunning, and you should read it.

Further Reading for This Chapter

Chait, J. (May 8, 2023). Indoctrination Nation: Convinced that schools are brainwashing kids to be left-wingers, conservatives seizing control of the American classroom. *New York Magazine* https://nymag.com/intelligencer/article/ desantis-florida-trump-education-politics.html

Lehrer-Small, A. (May 1, 2023). Texas Guts 'Woke' Civics. Now Kids Can't Participate in a Key Democratic Process. *The Guardian* https://www.theguardian.com/ us-news/2023/may/01/texas-civics-students-democratic-participation

Najarro, I. (May 2, 2023). Florida Pays Teachers $3K for Completing Civics Training. *EducationWeek.* https://www.edweek.org/teaching-learning/florida-pays -teachers-3k-for-completing-civics-training-how-it-compares-to-other -states/2023/05

Praise for *Democracy: A Love Letter*

"With wisdom, warmth, and humor, Clancy has put forth a practical guide for those looking to make meaningful change in their communities. Infused with the collective knowledge of activists from across the country, *Democracy: A Love Letter* offers a much-needed antidote to our era of political cynicism."

—**Marin Cogan,** senior correspondent at Vox

"This book will make you feel like an optimist about politics for the first time in your life."

—**Ashwini Habbu,** Austin, TX

"In these times when we feel so much has been lost, it is important to remember that we actually know how to win. When we organize and engage people inclusively and holistically, the arc of justice prevails. *Democracy: A Love Letter* is a succinct, practical, and empowering guide to applying proven organizing frameworks to (little-d) democracy itself."

—**Innosanto Nagara,** author of *A is for Activist, Oh, the Things We're For!* and other books for children of the 99%

"Saving democracy should not be some lofty, abstract idea that only matters to historians and political scientists. Saving democracy is the only way regular people like you and me can make sure our government works for us and responds to our daily needs. Deeply informed by conversation and collaboration with experts from across the country, Clancy entertains along the way as she shows us, invaluably, why we should care, what we can do about it, and, most importantly, why the right time is always now."

—**Justin Brannan,** New York City councilman

"In *Democracy: A Love Letter*, Kelly Clancy, PhD, takes readers on an inspiring journey through the resilient spirit of democracy. As a recently naturalized US citizen, an activist, and a recently registered voter, with this book, I have a roadmap for better mobilizing and organizing. It is an essential companion for anyone dedicated to making a meaningful impact in their communities. Clancy's passionate call to action will inspire you, as it did me, to embrace your role in shaping a more just and inclusive world. A compelling read for activists, dreamers, and all who believe in the power of democracy."

—**Abdi Iftin,** author of *Call Me American*

"In this book, Clancy outlines an ambitious vision for an inclusive democracy and gives practical advice on how to get there. *Democracy: A Love Letter* is a must-read for progressive activists, scholars of social change, and anyone who is concerned about the state of democracy today."

—**Brooke Foucault Welles,** co-author of *HashtagActivism: Networks of Race and Gender Justice*

"Envisioning a culture of continuous protest, where resistance isn't just occasional but something we incorporate into our daily lives, Clancy asks us to reimagine the democracy we want to live in—then organize and fight to make it a reality. This timely and conversational how-to guide for current (and would-be!) activists conveys a sense of optimism about what ordinary people can accomplish when they make collective demands from the powers that be."

—**Michael Levitin,** author of *Generation Occupy: Reawakening American Democracy*

ABOUT THE AUTHOR

Kelly A. Clancy is an award-winning writer living in Brooklyn with her husband, three kids, and giant orange cat. Before becoming a full-time writer, editor, and consultant, she was a tenured political science professor at a small liberal arts school in the Midwest. She has traveled globally from Bosnia to Belize to explore, study, and do research, and she thinks that New York City is the best place in the world to live and raise kids. Kelly holds a PhD in political science from Rutgers University.

kellyaclancy.com
www.savingtheworldbook.com

www.ingramcontent.com/pod-product-compliance
Lightning Source LLC
Chambersburg PA
CBHW070105030426
42335CB00016B/2019